Sozaboy

SOZABOY

A novel in rotten English

Ken Saro-Wiwa

Introduction by William Boyd
(author of *A Good Man in Africa*)

Pearson Education Limited
Edinburgh Gate Harlow,
Essex CM20 2JE, England
and Associated Companies throughout the world.

Longman Publishing Group
10 Bank Street
White Plains
New York 10601-1951
USA

Canadian stockist
Copp Clark Longman Ltd
2775 Matheson Blvd East
Mississauga
Ontario L4W 4P7
Canada

Nigerian edition published in 1985 by
Saros International Publishers, Port Harcourt,
Nigeria

First published in Longman African Writers 1994

14 13 12 11
19 18 17 16

British Library Cataloguing in Publication Data
A CIP record for this book is available from the British Library
East

Phototypeset by A.K.M. Associates (U.K.) Ltd
Ajmal House, Hayes Road, Southall, London

Printed in Malaysia, PPSB

ISBN 978-0-582-23699-8

'Although, everybody in Dukana was happy at first' is the wonderful and audacious opening line of a wonderful and audacious novel. By the novel's conclusion, however, this sentence's disarming grammar and its minatory simplicity (what does that "at first" portend?) have taken on more sinister and melancholy hues. One has learned that this is the beginning of a story about innocence brutally lost and of a consolatory wisdom only fleetingly and partially grasped. The incomprehension – and the profound sadness – is gathered there in those few words; the inspired, odd displacement of "Although" carries a new poignancy.

Sozaboy is a war novel, the narrative of one young man's helpless and hapless journey through a terrifying African war. Although – it is curious how the word has changed, somehow, charged with its *Sozaboy* freight – Ken Saro-Wiwa does not specify it is in fact set during a particular and precise conflict, namely the Nigerian civil war of 1967–1970, also known as the Biafran War. Unusually for an African conflict, it was one that figured prominently on British television screens. Nigeria was a former colony (independence had been granted seven years previously) and Britain had powerful vested interests there. The British government's support – material and diplomatic – was firmly behind the Federal Government, led by General Gowon, and against the secessionist eastern states, known as Biafra, led by General Ojukwu. There were no clear-cut heroes or villains in this conflict, and culpability can be equally distributed; but with hindsight one can see that the decision of the eastern states to secede made war – and also eventual defeat – inevitable. That the war lasted as long as it did, and that it caused as much misery and suffering (over a million died, mostly civilians, mostly from disease and starvation in the shrinking, blockaded heartland that was Biafra), is a result of many familiar factors: heroic tenacity, woeful stupidity, tactical blunders, difficult terrain, muddle and confusion, extended supply lines and so on. Anyone who requires an overview of this almost forgotten war should read *The Struggle for Secession* by N.U. Akpan, the best account that I know. Histories of the war are very thick on the ground or otherwise ponderously, not to say ludicrously, partisan; Nigerian novelists have been swifter off the mark and truer to this bleak chapter in their country's history, and there are fine and moving works of fiction by Chinua Achebe and Ben Okri (among others) which treat of the conflict. But in my opinion *Sozaboy* remains the war's enduring literary monument.

Ken Saro-Wiwa is from eastern Nigeria, a member of the Ogoni tribe. The outbreak of war in 1967 trapped him within the new boundaries of the Biafran state. It is important to establish that not all easterners wanted to secede from the Nigerian federation. General Ojukwu was an Ibo, the dominant tribe in Eastern Nigeria. When he declared Biafra independent, 'Ibo' and 'Biafra' were not at all synonymous: like it or not, some thirty or so other ethnic groups were included in the new country. Like it or not, these other tribes found themselves at war against Nigeria.

This fact explains much that is intentionally fuzzy about the novel. No one seems to understand why war is impending or why it breaks out. No one seems really sure why they are fighting or against whom: they are designated simply as 'the enemy'. To many eastern Nigerians caught up in the Biafran net, the motives for war and the nature of their adversaries must have seemed equally vague. Sozaboy – as the hero, Mene, is dubbed ('Soza' means 'soldier') – is one such uncertain conscript and he meanders through the novel in an almost permanent state of ignorance; clarity beckoning from time to time only to be occluded promptly. This is a state of mind familiar to all front-line soldiers, but to the many non-Ibos dragooned into the Biafran army there must have been an extra degree of obfuscation.

Ken Saro-Wiwa was one who perceived the absurdity and injustice of fighting another man's secessionist war. He escaped through the front lines to the federal side and was appointed civilian administrator of the crucial oil-port of Bonny on the Niger River delta (he has written of his own experiences in the civil war in his fine autobiography, *On a Darkling Plain*), where he served until the final collapse of the secessionist forces, marked by the flight of General Ojukwu to the Ivory Coast in January 1970. I lived in Nigeria during the Biafran war and can testify to the novel's authentic feel. The war did seem that crazy, that surreal and haphazard. But any reader will experience the same undeniable reek of life as it comes off the page. *Sozaboy* is vivid with the special authority of personal experience.

It is also vivid with a language of uncommon idiosyncrasy and character. Saro-Wiwa subtitles the novel as 'A Novel in Rotten English'. Rotten English, as he explains, is a blend of pidgin English (the lingua franca of the West-African ex-colonies), corrupted English and 'occasional flashes of good, even idiomatic English'. In other words, the language of the novel is a unique literary construct. No one in Nigeria actually speaks or writes like this but the style functions in the novel extraordinarily well. Sozaboy's narration is at times raunchily funny as well as lyrical and moving, and as the terror of his predicament steadily manifests itself, the small but colourful vocabulary of his idiolect paradoxically manages to capture all the numbing ghastliness of war far more effectively than a more expansive eloquence. It helps to hear the rhythms of a Nigerian accent in your ear as you read, but even if that cannot be reproduced, the cadences of the prose take over after a few lines or so and this remarkable tone of voice holds the reader's attention absolutely. Some obscure words or phrases are explained in a glossary, but one is never in any doubt about that is going on, and the sheer freshness and immediacy of the subjective point of view are exhilarating. Here Sozaboy visits a local dive:

> So, one night, after I have finished bathing, I put powder and scent and went to African Upwine Bar. This African Upwine Bar is in interior part of Diobu. Inside inside. We used to call this Diobu New York. I think you know New York. In America. As people plenty for am, na so dem plenty for Diobu too. Like cockroach. And true true cockroach plenty for Diobu too. Everywhere, like the men. And if you go inside the African Upwine Bar you will see plenty cockroach man and proper cockroach too. Myself, I like the African Upwine bar. Because you fit drink better palmy there. Fine palmy of three or four days old.

This mode of literary demotic is a highly impressive achievement. Saro-Wiwa has both invented and captured a voice here, one not only bracingly authentic but also capable of many fluent and telling registers. I cannot think of another example where the English language has been so engagingly and skilfully hijacked –

or perhaps 'colonised' would be a better word. Indeed, throughout the novel, Saro-Wiwa exploits Rotten English with delicate and consummate skill. We see everything through Sozaboy's naive eyes, and his hampered vision – even in the face of the most shocking sights – is reproduced through inevitable understatement. Sozaboy's vocabulary simply cannot encompass the strange concepts he encounters or the fearful enormity of what he is undergoing. Yet these silences, these occlusions and fumblings for expression exert a marvellous power. Here a fifth-columnist has been undermining the new recruits' shaky morale:

> So that night Manmuswak did not spend long time with us. After some time he told us that we must be careful because nobody can know when the war will come reach our front. So we told him goodnight, and he began to go away, small small like tall snake passing through the bush, making small noise.

The threat of impending disaster has never been more economically or chillingly conveyed.

Sozaboy's nightmare picaresque begins when, full of zeal to impress his new wife Agnes, he decides to join up and become a 'Soza'. It is the uniform he is really after, hungry for the esteem it will confer on him in his village, where he is only an apprentice lorry driver. The downward spiral of his fortunes in the army – boredom, mutiny, punishment, battle and capture – depress and mortify him, but he somehow never loses his fundamental ebullience, his innocent *joie de vivre*. He reminds me of another classic of African literature, Mr Johnson in Joyce Cary's novel of the same name. Like Mr Johnson, Sozaboy knows shame and humiliation, and like Mr Johnson it is his resilient spirit and the thought of his young wife that spur him on to greater endeavours no matter what desperate straits he finds himself in. But Sozaboy is also an African Candide and this is where Ken Saro-Wiwa's novel takes on dimensions that are absent in Joyce Cary's. Mr Johnson is a great character, as is Sozaboy, but – like Voltaire's Candide – Sozaboy is also an archetype and a victim in a way that Mr Johnson is not. Malign forces pluck up up Sozaboy, whirl him around and deposit him in a heap, his spirit almost crushed, his village ruined, his family slaughtered, his prospects negligible. One needs only to glance at the recent history of Africa to see how paradigmatic Sozaboy's story is: young men in uniforms, clutching their AK47s, spread fear and desolation, march and die all over the continent.

At the novel's end, Sozaboy contemplates the destruction that has been wreaked on his life and reflects:

> I was thinking how I was prouding before to go to soza and call myself Sozaboy. But now if anybody say anything about war or even fight, I will just run and run and run and run and run. Believe me yours sincerely.

Heartfelt and timeless thoughts, any simple bathos undercut by the astute final sentence, where the half-remembered formal valediction (the words are vapid and empty at the end of a letter) takes on an unfamiliar fervency and gravitas in its new and bitter context.

Sozaboy is a novel born out of harsh personal experience, but shaped with a masterful and sophisticated artistry despite its apparent rough-hewn guilelessness. With equal skill and deftness, it also carries a profound moral message that extends beyond its particular time and setting. Sozaboys are legion, and their lives are being destroyed everywhere on the planet. *Sozaboy* is not simply a great African novel, it is also a great anti-war novel, among the very best the twentieth century has produced.

William Boyd
London
February 1994

AUTHOR'S NOTE

Twenty years ago, at Ibadan University, I wrote a story titled 'High Life' and showed it to one of my teachers, Mr. O.R. Dathorne. He read it, just possibly liked it; but he did say that while the style I had used might be successful in a short story, he doubted that it could be sustained in a novel. I knew then that I would have to write a novel, some day, in the same style. The Nigerian Civil War which I saw from very close quarters among young soldiers in Bonny where I was civilian Administrator, provided me with the right opportunity.

Mr. Dathorne later published 'High Life' in a collection, *Africa in Prose* Penguin African Library (1969). The entry against it runs thus '. . . the piece is not in true 'Pidgin' which would have made it practically incomprehensible to the European reader. The language is that of a barely educated primary school boy exulting in the new words he is discovering and the new world he is beginning to know.' Mr. Dathorne goes on to describe the style in the story as 'an uninhibited gamble with language', and 'an exercise in an odd style'.

Both 'High Life' and *Sozaboy* are the result of my fascination with the adaptability of the English Language and of my closely observing the speech and writings of a certain segment of Nigerian society. For, As Platt, Weber and Ho accurately observe in their book, *The New Englishes*, (RKP 1984) 'In some nations . . . the New Englishes have developed a noticeable range of different varieties linked strongly to the socio-economic and educational backgrounds of their speakers.'

Sozaboy's language is what I call 'rotten English', a mixture of Nigerian pidgin English, broken English and occasional flashes of good, even idiomatic English. This language is disordered and disorderly. Born of a mediocre education and severely limited opportunities, it borrows words, patterns and images freely from the mother-tongue and finds expression in a very limited English vocabulary. To its speakers, it has the advantage of having no rules and no syntax. It thrives on lawlessness, and is part of the dislocated and discordant society in which Sozaboy must live, move and have not his being.

Whether it throbs vibrantly enough and communicates effectively is my experiment.

Ken Saro-Wiwa   Port Harcourt   1985

For my father, Chief J.B. Wiwa (1904–)
with love and gratitude.

LOMBER ONE

Although, everybody in Dukana was happy at first.

All the nine villages were dancing and we were eating plenty maize with pear and knacking tory under the moon. Because the work on the farm have finished and the yams were growing well well. And because the old, bad government have dead, and the new government of soza and police have come.

Everybody was saying that everything will be good in Dukana because of new government. They were saying that *kotuma ashbottom* from Bori cannot take bribe from people in Dukana again. They were saying too that all those policemen who used to chop big big bribe from people who get case will not chop again. Everybody was happy because from that time, even magistrate in the court at Bori will begin to give better judgement. And traffic police will do his work well well. Even one woman was talking that the sun will shine proper proper and people will not die again because there will be medicine in the hospital and the doctor will not charge money for operation. Yes, everybody in Dukana was happy. And they were all singing.

Me too. Because as young man and apprentice driver, they will not give us too much trouble on the road again. Because, before, if you want to take licence, you will pay money to the clerk who will give you the form. Then you must pay money to another clerk who will write inside the book. Then when you take your lorry for driving test, you must pay very big money to VIO. Then you can get your licence whether you sabi drive or you no sabi.

My master used to say that they are all tiefman. All of them. Because not so government tell them to do. And they are all chopping bribe from the small small people. My master say it is very bad at all. So we were all very happy when they talk that it will stop now that there is new government of soza and police.

Before before, even if your motor full oh or 'e no full, you must give traffic at least ten shillings for morning and ten shillings for evening return journey. Inspector Okonkwo na him be the worst when he was sarzent before they promoted him. He chopped bribe from drivers until he can be able to marry four wives and build better house for his town. Even, when they promote him to Inspector, my master and myself went to *gratulate* him. But lo and behold, when we reach there now, Inspector Okonkwo was crying. He was crying with water from his eye. No joke oh. I have not seen such kain thing before. How can person who get promotion begin to cry? Instead of to be happy. When my master ask Okonkwo why 'e dey cry, Okonkwo said:

"Smog," – that is how he used to call my master, – "Smog, how I no go cry? Look my house. Fridge, radiogram, carpet, four wives; better house for my village. You tink say na my salary I use for all dese things? If I no stand for road dere to be traffic you tink say I for fit? Ah, dis promotion, na demotion. Make dem take de Inspector, give me my sarzent."

My master was laughing small small, with his fat body shaking. Then he told Okonkwo to not to worry. Because Inspector too can share any bribe money which sarzent and constable bring. Inspector Okonkwo tell my master make 'e lef am for God. Because him know how much sarzent dey get and how much 'e dey show to Inspector. Then he began to cry again.

Well, all these things were confusing me. When people say that better government have come and there will be no more bribe, I begin to wonder whether Inspector Okonkwo will not be there again. But my master told me that Okonkwo is bigger bigger man in new government than before sef. And still they talk that there will be no more bribe again. Well, we go sit down look.

Anyway, to talk true, there was no bribe for some time. But

after some time they begin again. The traffic begin with small small bribe. Then they increased it by small. Until they begin to take bigger bigger bribe than before. Then the people begin to say that now wey soza and police be government, nobody can be able to arrest traffic when they chop bribe. Because government cannot arrest government. So therefore, everything will be okay for the big big people who are chopping the bribe.

So, although everyone was happy at first, after some time, everything begin to spoil small by small and they were saying that trouble have started. People were not happy to hear that there is trouble everywhere. Everywhere the people were talking about it. In Pitakwa. In Bori. And in Dukana. Radio begin dey hala as 'e never hala before. Big big grammar. Long long words. Every time.

Before before, the grammar was not plenty and everybody was happy. But now grammar begin to plenty and people were not happy. As grammar plenty, na so trouble plenty. And as trouble plenty, na so plenty people were dying.

We people cannot understand plenty what was happening. But the radio and other people were talking of how people were dying. And plenty people were returning to their village. From far far places. We motor people begin to make plenty money. Plenty trouble, plenty money. And my master was prouding. Making *yanga* for all the people, all the time. We were charging passengers as lawyer used to charge people who get case. Heavy. People were returning. We were charging them proper. My master say if it continues like this, we can buy new motor very soon.

In the motor park, the returning people were saying many things. I heard plenty tory by that time. About how they are killing people in the train; cutting their hand or their leg or breaking their head with matchet or chooking them with spear and arrow. Fear begin catch me small. Soon, everybody begin to fear. Why all this trouble now? Ehn? Why? Even for Dukana fear begin to catch everybody.

The radio continue to blow big big grammar, talking big talk. We continue to make big money, my master and myself. Everybody was afraid, but things continue as before. For the farm. And for market. No trouble in Dukana or in Bori or in Pitakwa. Only some time people will gather round to talk about what they have heard. And everybody was saying what entered his mind whether it is true oh or it is not true.

Pastor Barika of Church of Light of God, the most important church in Dukana, was saying that the world will soon end. I no like that one at all. How will the world end and I never get my licence? Is that good thing? How will world end and I never marry sef? This Pastor Barika is useless man. I don't like as he was talking all that nonsense. He is useless man inside useless church. I know it, but I cannot tell him. I just keep quiet.

Chief Birabee, the king of Dukana, he was the most afraid. He is old man with bald head. Not completely bald-oh. It is like bird have been chopping his hair. And he does not comb the one that remained. Everyday in the evening when we return from Pitakwa, he will ask me what is happening. When I answer that it is nothing, he will ask again whether I am sure. I will say yes. Then he will beat his snuff box and say that I am stupid. Very stupid. How can I say that nothing is happening whereas man of God like Pastor Barika have seen vision that the world will soon end?

I say to myself that Chief Birabee is very coward man. As old man why will he begin to fear if the world will soon end? Will old man not die whether there is trouble or no trouble? Anyway, Chief Birabee is very afraid. So he likes to call meeting of Dukana elders to ask what is happening and what he will do.

However, I don't think that anybody can help him, because all those people in Dukana do not know anything. Dukana is far away from any better place in this world. You must go far in motor before you can get to Pitakwa. All the houses in the town are made of mud. There is no good road or drinking water. Even the school is not fine and no hospital or anything. The people of Dukana are fishermen and farmers. They no know anything more than fish and farm. Radio sef they no get. How can they know what is happening? Even myself who travel every day to Pitakwa, township with plenty brick house and running water and electric, I cannot understand what is happening well well, how much less all these simple people tapping palm wine and making fisherman, planting yam and cassava in Dukana? So Chief Birabee is in trouble.

And his trouble was more than when government passed message that no person should dance again and beat drum because of the trouble. And then the government begin to ask the people to do many other things. And the people were very unhappy.

One night, the town-crier begin to beat drum throughout Dukana. I just return from work and I tire plenty, so I was lying down after my chop. The town-crier begin to hala. 'E say na so the chief talk. Tomorrow, nobody will go to work. Whether big man or small man. Nobody will go. Everybody will report early in the morning to the town square because the chief want to talk to everybody there.

In Dukana, anytime you hear that everybody is to meet in the town square you must begin to fear. Because either there is work on the road or they want to collect money which the chiefs will chop. Nobody for Dukana like to work on the road. Worst still to collect money. Because all the money the people collect is not used proper. So if you hear that there is meeting in the town square, you must run away before morning time. But the chiefs have known that cunny now. So therefore, they will always block every road from the town in the night before the town-crier begin to cry round the town.

When my master heard that they have blocked the road, he was very angry. He came to my mama house to see me.

"What kain nonsense be dis?" is what he said. "Plenty money for road and dem begin to block de road. Wetin de chiefs mean? Dem no want make I chop?"

I beg him to not to worry because passengers will not finish for road.

"Not finish for road? Is it not because people are running now that there are passengers for road? Will they not finish? Have I make so much money in one year as I make for dis week alone? Oh, dese chiefs are useless people. Why can they be stupid like dis? Anyway, na dem get the lorry. Make dem do anything dem want. Which one concern me? Nonsense."

I see that my master is very angry but sleep don dey catch me. My master come go. I begin to sleep on the mat on the floor. I sleep well well too. Because the floor is better than bench in moving lorry in which I used to sleep when I am on duty.

When I opened my eye, day have begin to break. Light everywhere. I jump up and begin to roll the mat. Then I put the mat under my armpit. Then I run to where we park the lorry. Lo and behold, as I am walking to the lorry, plenty people are hurrying to the town square. Man. Woman. Children. Everybody. Some tie cloth. Some no get shirt sef. Some were using chewing stick, spitting along the road. Some women carried their baby for back. All of them were going to listen to what the chief will say. Myself, I followed them. Because I must follow when the chief call.

Everybody was standing in the town square. Except Chief Birabee and the elders. They were sitting down. They were not smiling. Serious like boxer.

"Ha!" I say to myself, "trouble dey for country."

So we were all standing there, waiting and waiting.

The sun never appear yet. Every place cool like forest. Water fall from all the trees and plantain and grass everywhere. Good. Then Chief Birabee stood up and begin to speak. First, he cough. Kpuhu! Kpuhu! His face was still very serious. Haba! What kain trouble be dis? Then he began to speak, as I hear 'am.

"My people, listen to me very carefully. As all of you know, there is plenty trouble now. True, the trouble never reach Dukana yet. But plenty of trouble dey all the same. Everywhere in our country. Government no like trouble. So therefore, nobody here must give trouble. At all. Because Dukana people do not give trouble since the world begin. Now, Government say we must give money, chop and cloth to all those who run home. Because we are good people, we must respect and obey government. Everybody. Man. Woman. Picken. Anybody who get money, chop or cloth must bring it. We go give am to those porsons wey just return. Is not byforce, oh. We cannot byforce anybody. That is what government talk. But as you all know, government cannot talk say it will byforce anybody. But government is government. And although government will not talk that it is byforcing anyone, still it will byforce. So therefore, we must try to find all those things that government is asking for."

6

Duzia spoke first. Everybody know that Duzia will speak first. Duzia is always like that. Because he cannot walk. Since he was born. Duzia is cripple man. But the man na one kain man. He must always talk first in Dukana. Duzia knows everything. Everything. About Dukana. About the world. And he must always talk. So after the Chief, Duzia spoke first. He was sitting on that cold ground. No shirt for him body, sef. So he began to speak, as I hear 'am.

"I greet the Chiefs. I greet the elders. I greet the rich. I greet the poor. I greet the brave. I greet the coward. I greet everybody. Well, me, I do not get plenty sense. But I get small sense. Even if I do not have money, I get small sense which God give me. Chief Birabee, we have heard what you have said. It is good. You say make we no give trouble. Awright. We cannot give trouble. We people in Dukana do not give trouble. We never give trouble before. So we cannot begin to give trouble now. Even all the trouble which you say plenty for the country we don't know about it. At all. Na you dey tell us. And you are Chief. So we must to believe you".

Everybody begin to laugh small laugh.

"So as I was saying, we must to believe you. But there is one part which I no like and which I cannot like. I say I no get plenty sense and I no get money, but I must speak what is worrying my mind. I think you are all hearing what I am saying? How can porson like myself without house, without wife, without farm, without cloth to wear begin to give money, chop and cloth to government? Not government dey give chop and money and cloth to porson? Now porson go begin give government chop? Awright. You talk say government fit byforce porson to give them all wey dem want. Government go fit byforce porson like me to give anything?"

Everybody begin to laugh small small. But Duzia never finish yet.

"Awright, they fit come take these legs wey I no get."

By this time, everybody don dey laugh well well.

"Awright, awright", the town people begin to hala.

"Whasmatter with you people? Can't you shut your mouth? You want fly to fall inside? Small thing and you begin to form-fool". That is what the headmaster of Dukana school was saying.

But the people cannot keep quiet. They continue to laugh and talk. From what they were saying I know that many people do not like what Chief Birabee have said. Because Dukana people no get money and they no get property. So they cannot like to give anything to another porson whether na byforce or not byforce.

"How can porson give something to government? When we have paid tax finish, then they begin to ask for dash again. Na good government so?" Bom said.

The noise in the square plenty by now.

Chief Birabee stood up again. "*Odah, odah,*" he shouted. "Listen to me my people. I don't want you people to confuse yourself. You may be thinking, oh, it is Chief Birabee who want to chop your money, wear your cloth, drink your *tombo.* I am telling you that it is not so. At all. What I told you before and what I am telling you now is government word. Myself, I do not want palaver. I do not want government to come here now and begin to arrest people with *kotuma* and police. That will make plenty palaver and *wuruwuru* will begin. That is not what I want in Dukana. I want peace. And anything that will bring peace, I must to do."

Everybody was quiet. Some people begin to confuse. Nobody want to hear of *kotuma* worst still, police in Dukana. If they see police sef, everyone will begin to run go inside bush or farm to hide. So when Birabee began to talk police and kotuma that morning, everyone was afraid. All the men. Women do not talk in Dukana meeting. Anything the men talk, the women must do. Dukana people say woman does not get mouth. And it is true.

As the people have begin to fear now and even Duzia no fit talk again, I see that Chief Birabee have win. He began to laugh small for him mouth. Then he began to give order. He said every man must bring three shillings and every woman one shilling. With that money, government will be happy and everything will be awright.

Many of the men do not like what Chief Birabee have said. "What" they asked, "not woman get money pass man? How can man pay more than woman? That is not good. Nonsense. Woman can get money from man easy. And woman works hard. Yet when time to collect money reach they will begin to ask man to pay more than woman. Nonsense."

But Chief Birabee does not want to listen again. He began to walk away. Everybody begin to go. From what they were saying as we were going home, I can see that they do not understand what Chief Birabee have said. All they are thinking is how they will pay the three three and one one shilling. Many people do not like it. They think it is Chief Birabee and his friends who will chop all the money. The women too begin to complain and grumble. They were cursing Chief Birabee. "Stupid Chief. Stupid tief. When they cannot find something to eat, they begin to move around the town looking for small tax to collect. Stupid tiefs."

As for myself, to pay three shillings cannot hard apprentice driver. Everyday I must get more than three shillings and I no count my chop money sef. So three shillings is nothing. What is worrying me is what Chief Birabee is saying. That government say there is plenty of trouble everywhere. People are returning and we must give them chop. Well, I cannot understand at all. But I fear small. Even, I fear plenty. Suppose as Pastor Barika is saying, actually world will end because of the trouble, then what will happen? I never marry. My mama go vex with me because I never marry yet and world don begin to end. And I never get licence although I can drive quite well. What will I tell my God when I return?

Anyway, why the trouble? Ehn? Why the trouble? Wetin bring the trouble? Ehn? Jesus my lord. Can you not take this trouble away? So I was speaking like this to myself until I reached home. I begin to think what I will do if the trouble come reach Dukana. But I cannot think too much about that one now, otherwise trouble go begin. I go begin to confuse myself and everybody. When I ask my master what he think about as Chief Birabee was talking, he told me not to worry. Chief Birabee is only looking for money to chop. How can government ask man to give am chop and cloth and money?

Anyway, Chief Birabee and him people begin take money from every man and woman. Man three shillings. Woman one shilling. The people no happy to pay. They are cursing as they are paying. Chief Birabee does not bother. He was saying that he will take police to hold anyone who does not agree to pay. The people of Dukana were not happy at all.

But that one no concern me. My master and myself continue to go Pitakwa and return. Some times we will go two times in one day. Plenty passenger for road, plenty money. We were doing like that until the lorry come spoil. O–oh! So I do not go Dukana again. I have to stay with the lorry in Pitakwa should in case they finish repairing it quick quick and then work can begin again.

LOMBER TWO

I am free-born of Dukana and that is where I went to school. I am the only son of my mama and I have no father. It is my mama who sent me to St.Dominic's school in Dukana where I passed my elementary six with distinction. In fact, I am very clever boy in school and I like to work hard always. It was very hard for my mama to pay my school fees but she tried hard to make me finish in that school.

When I passed the elementary six exam, I wanted to go to secondary school but my mama told me that she cannot pay the fees. The thing pained me bad bad because I wanted to be big man like lawyer or doctor riding car and talking big big English. In fact I used to know English in the school and every time I will try to read any book that I see. So when I see that I cannot go secondary, I was not happy. However, that is my luck.

So my mama told me that I should learn to be driver. Because Dukana people have one lorry which they call 'Progres'. But they have no driver and they have to go and get driver from another country to drive the lorry. And this driver is very rich man because he gets salary every month and every day he must get chop money. And the lorry is his house so he does not spend money to get house. My mama say that if I am apprentice to this driver, after some time I will get my own licence and then I can get my own lorry to drive. And if I save my salary and my chop money, I can buy my own lorry and then I will be big man like any lawyer or doctor. So I like that and after we have paid money to the driver of 'Progres' plus one goat and one bottle of Gordon gin and one piece of cloth, I become his apprentice.

Every day, early in the morning, 'Progres' must leave Dukana very early with passenger and it will stop in every village to collect more passengers till it reach Bori where we will stop for chop and then we will continue till we reach Pitakwa. There we will stop in the motor park and then all the passengers will come down. We will wait there till afternoon when the passengers have bought all their goods and then they will enter 'Progres' and when they are plenty or they have full the lorry, we will return to Dukana. Always we must reach Dukana before night time unless something is wrong.

I myself as apprentice driver in 'Progres', I am prouding plenty. Because I take my work serious. And as I am going to Pitakwa every day, I am learning new new things. In the motor park, I must speak English with the other drivers and apprentice and passengers. Even some time I will see all those small small books that they are selling in the park. And as I used to get chop money every day, I will use some of the money to buy the books and improve my English. So I was getting money and learning plenty things.

I have been doing this apprentice driver work for two years before the trouble in the country began. By that time, I already know everything about the motor and I can even drive and change tyre and put water in the engine. And I like the work. It remain just one year for me to go for test to get my licence. I know that when I get the licence I will be prouding in Dukana as first driver from Dukana concern.

When the lorry spoils, we must send it to the garage. And when the lorry is in the garage, there is no work for my master and myself. Then I can do anything that I want. But I must stay in Pitakwa. In the morning, I will go to motor park to load other people motor. By that, I can be able to make small money that I will use to buy chop. Because if motor spoils, then my master cannot give me chop money from his pocket.

If I can make small money for morning time, I will chop groundnut and sometimes I will drink ice water in the motor park. But I know that I will eat properly only in the night.

In the night, I will wash myself, comb my hair and put

powder and some small Bint-el-Sudan scent. Then I will wear better cloth too and go to any Bar that I like. I must wear better cloth when I am going out in the night because when I go out I can meet some fine baby and although driver work look like dirty work, it is not so. Driver work is good work and drivers must preserve their persy all the time. Otherwise someone can start to mess up their senior commando. As driver, the same for apprentice driver.

So, one night after I have finished bathing, I put powder and scent and went to African Upwine Bar. This African Upwine Bar is in interior part of Diobu. Inside inside. We use to call this Diobu New York. I think you know New York. In America. As people plenty for am. Na so dem plenty for Diobu. Like cockroach. And true true cockroach plenty for Diobu too. Everywhere. Like the men. And if you go inside the African Upwine Bar, you will see plenty cockroach man and proper cockroach too. Myself, I like the African Upwine Bar. Because you fit drink better palmy there. Fine palmy of three or four days old. And there are fine babies there too. And you can chop *okporoko*, stockfish. Or *ngwo-ngwo*, goat-head and particulars in pepper soup. And it will not cost you plenty money.

They used to call this African Upwine Bar 'Mgbaijiji', which mean to say the place can bring plenty fly. True, if you enter the Bar in the morning time or afternoon time, the fly will not allow you to chop or drink. They will be falling inside your palmy. But in the night, all the flies don sleep. They sleep on the wall and nothing can wake them from sleep.

So that night, I was in the Upwine Bar. No plenty people at first. I order one bottle of palmy from the service. This service is young girl. Him bottom dey shake as she walk. Him breast na proper J.J.C, Johnny Just Come – dey stand like hill. As I look am, my man begin to stand small small. I beg am make 'e no disgrace me especially as I no wear pant that night. I begin to drink my palmy. The service sit near my table dey look me from the corner of him eye. Me I dey look am too with the corner of my eye. I want see how him breast dey. As I dey look, the baby catch me.

"What are you looking at?" is what she asked.

"I am not looking at anything," was my answer.

"But why are you looking at me with corner-corner eye?" she asked again.

"Look you for corner-corner eye? Why I go look you for corner-corner eye?" was my answer.

"You dey look my breast, *yeye* man. Make you see am now".

Before I could twinkle my eye, lo and behold she have moved her dress and I see her two breasts like calabash. God in Heaven. What kain thing be this? *Abi*, the girl no dey shame? Small time, the girl don put back him breast for him cloth. I drink my *tombo*, super palm wine.

"Make I play you music?" was what she asked next.

"Okay. I like music."

"Which kain music?"

"Music get kain? Just play me any record. I think you get record in this bar?"

"Plenty. But is there any record wey you like plenty?"

"No. I like congo and I like highlife. Especially highlife."

"Awright. I go play you 'Ashewo'. I think you know 'Ashewo'?"

I was beginning to shame. How can this young girl be speaking like this to me? Abi, the girl no dey shame? Anyway, I must not show that I shame pass woman. So I tell her "Yes, I know *ashewo*. Play it for me."

So she put the record. Na Rex Lawson record. I stand up to dance. The service follow me to dance. I was holding her and she was holding me too. Very tight. My man was standing up.

"Are you hungry?" was what the baby asked me as we were dancing.

"No," was my answer.

"Are you sure?" she asked me again.

"Oh yes."

"Awright. But make you tell your snake make 'e no too stand like say 'e dey hungry."

I am telling you, this kain talk can make me shame. Since they born me I have never hold woman like I hold that service that night. Even woman never tell me what that baby was telling me. Shame catch me. I cannot talk again. I continue to dance but my dance not like dance again.

"Are you tired? Can't you dance again?" was what she asked me.

I cannot answer. By that time, some people entered the bar and the service must go and attend them. So she rubbed my face with her hand and told me not to go away.

I returned to my seat in the bar and she went and brought me another bottle of *tombo* wine. This *tombo* was special. It was sweeter than all other *tombo* that I have drink before. There is no water in it. I begin to think that I am lucky man after all. Why is Pastor Barika talking that the world will soon end?

"Oh yes, the world will soon end."

Ah – ah, I was frightened. At first I think that it is Pastor Barika. But no. It is the men who entered the bar just now. They were sitting on the small table near me.

"Yes, the world will end this year," that is what the tall man was saying.

"You think so?" the short man was asking.

"Sure sure."

The tall man was drinking his own tombo from the bottle.

"How can the world not end? Have you seen such wickedness before? Man kill man. Man kill woman. Haba. Too much trouble now. Small time now the world go end."

"But why dem dey kill now?" Na so the short man ask.

"I can't know. My own is to drink. If I die tomorrow . . ."

"Mamy water go bury you," the short man say.

The two of them begin to laugh.

Then they begin to sing

> Mamy water go bury me
> If I die tomorrow
> If I die tomorrow
> If I die tomorrow
> Mamy water go bury me
> If I die tomorrow.

Small time, they get up and begin to dance. They are singing and dancing. Singing and dancing. Making plenty of noise in the house.

The service play the grammaphone and come to sit near me.

"What is your name?" she asked me.

"Mene".

"What work you do?"

"I am apprentice driver but I know how to drive now although I never get the licence yet".

I was prouding of that statement.

"You are a small boy," was what she answered.

I begin to shame. After some time, I do not shame again. I begin to angry. How can small girl like this with J.J.C. begin to call me small boy?

"Are you calling me small boy because I tell you that I am apprentice driver?"

She laugh. And laugh again.

"No. I think you are small boy because of how your snake was standing when I begin to dance with you. You never dance with woman before? When I show you my breast you begin to swallow saliva."

I do not know what I can say again. This girl want to make me look like stupid man.

"Where you come from?" was what I asked her after that.

"From Lagos," was her answer.

"Lagos? Ah, Lagos. No wonder you smart like this. So na Lagos you are living before?"

"Oh yes."

"But why you return home?"

"You no hear wetin dey happen? They were killing plenty people so I return home."

"Did you see anybody wey they kill?" was my next question.

"As for myself I do not see anybody. But they were saying that they will kill porson. So I packed all my things and run away."

"Is it true that plenty trouble dey for the country?"

"Well, na so I hear. But me, all I want now is how I will find my mama."

"Your mama?" I ask am. "You don't know where is your mama?"

"At all."

"You no live with am for Lagos?"

"No. I live by myself".

"By yourself? Why? Where is your mother?"

"I lef my mother long time ago."

"You know where she is living now?"

"Yes. I hear that she is in Dukana."

"Dukana?" I almost jump up. "You mean you are Dukana girl?"

"Yes. I was born in Dukana. My mama still living there. But my papa don die."

"So you are freeborn of Dukana?"

"Yes," she answered and went away to answer the call which one customer was calling her. I looked her well as she was walking away. She walked with style. She is not like all these stupid girls in Diobu, New York. She is neat and beautiful. And slender like palm tree. I think I like her very much. True. I like 'am. God in Heaven. And she is Dukana girl. Oh, I will marry her. But what about the trouble in the country?

"Well, the only trouble is that there is trouble. And we must fight. I hear them talk it on the radio." The tall man was sitting down again and singing and dancing and he was talking again as he was eating *okporoko* and drinking *tombo*. "Everyday they hala about it. Many people have dead. Therefore some more people must to die again."

"And you think it is good thing?" the short man was asking.

"Well, I don't think it is good thing or bad thing. Even sef I don't want to think. What they talk, we must do. Myself, if they say fight, I fight. If they say no fight, I cannot fight. Finish."

"But is it good thing to fight?" the short man was asking as he chopped *ngwongwo* from the plate.

"I like to fight. Yes. It is good thing to fight. If somebody take your thing by force, if 'e want byforce you to do something wey you no like to do, then you fit fight am."

"Well, as for myself, I like to chop *ngwongwo* and drink *tombo*. Anything that will disturb me and stop enjoyment, I cannot like it."

That is what the short man said as he drank another glass of *tombo* and chopped *ngwongwo* and belched one big belch – etiee! I begin to think of what those two men were saying. I think I agree small with the short man. But I no too sure. I cannot too sure.

"But you don fight before?" the short man was asking.

"No."

"You don see fight before?"

"Yes. I see people dey fight for market and for motor park every day."

"Na that kain fight radio talk say we go fight?"

"I think so," was what the tall man replied.

"Well," the short man answered and keep quiet, and drank his *tombo*. The tall man drank his *tombo* and chopped his *ngwongwo* too. Then he said:

"Praps the fight will strong pass the fight in motor park. Praps they will use gun and bomb and rifle. It does not matter. Fight is fight and war is war. Anytime it comes, I am ready."

The grammaphone was still playing. After 'ashewo', it began to play 'bottom belly'. Everything in that hotel was sweeting me. Especially the young baby who was making service. I tell you, I like baby who do not shame. And she come show me her calabash breast. Praps the girl love me oh. Ha! ha! Praps she love me. And na Dukana girl. But why 'e dey talk like that? Snakes and all. Snake. I like that name. I call it 'man' or 'prick' before. But the girl call am 'snake'. Ha! ha! ha! I begin to laugh. This girl na *waya*, oh.

The girl come near me now. The tall man and the short man finish to drink and they begin to go. The grammaphone stop. The baby come to sit near me.

"Look baby," I call am, "wetin be your name?"

"Wetin you go take my name do?"

"But I don tell you my name."

"Wetin be your name?" she asked.

"Na Mene. And your own?"

"Agnes."

"Agnes. Na good name. Na English name. I like am." And I like the girl. She is Dukana girl.

"Where do you come from," was what she asked me after that.

"I am from Dukana."

"Dukana? Are you from Dukana?"

"Oh yes," I answered, prouding plenty. "I am a freeborn of Dukana. It is my own very village."

18

"So you are my brother, my own brother."

"Oh yes." I was very very happy. This fine girl is calling me her brother.

"Tell me, how is everything in Dukana?"

"Everything fine. We are very happy there. Only all this talk of trouble dey make everyone begin to fear."

"You, wetin you think of the trouble?"

That question confuse me small. 'E confuse me, I tell you, because it is this young girl Agnes who is asking me. Before now, I just hear people talking trouble trouble. I do not think about it. When the tall man talk that he will fight although before he say he like to eat only, I confuse small. But when the short man say he does not like trouble, I begin to confuse again. Now that Agnes ask me what I think of the trouble, I know that trouble don begin. Because if I begin to think of the trouble I cannot do anything again. It was the trouble that made my master and myself to make plenty money until the motor get small accident and trouble. So the trouble only mean more work and better money for me and my master. And the trouble bring small money for Chief Birabee because that money which he is collecting for government he must chop some part of it. So when Agnes ask me wetin I think of the trouble, I confuse small. I don't know what I will say. I just say the first thing which I remember.

"Trouble no dey ring bell," was what I said.

Agnes begin laugh. I think that I tell her something stupid. Agnes laugh again, and me, I join am. Then I ask am what 'e think of the trouble.

Agnes make quick reply: "When trouble come, I like strong, brave man who can fight and defend me."

Then we two laughed again. By that time the drink don begin turn-turn for my eye. I ask Agnes which time she will come to Dukana. She say as soon as possible. I tell her that I like her to come quick because I like her very much and people of Dukana will glad to see her because they have not seen her for long time and because she is beautiful girl and smart and Dukana people will be prouding because one their daughter who have gone to Lagos have returned. So she told me that she will come to Dukana soon.

That night as I was going home, I was thinking what a beautiful world. Even Diobu that used to smell urine urine and dirty begin to smell good again. I was prouding plenty, whistling 'bottom belly' as I was walking along the road that night. I begin to think what lucky man I am. Soon I will get my licence. And then I can marry better baby who have travelled to Lagos. Not just Lagos baby, oh. Because Lagos baby can be useless. Plenty people go don sleep with am. And she will be useless. But Agnes na proper J.J.C. I think she will be very good wife. My mama will like her. But why is she talking of snake and showing her breast like that? And why she play that *ashewo* record? Is she *ashewo* too? Oh nonsense. Agnes cannot be *ashewo*. She is good girl. And when I get my licence and I marry her, then I get lorry and I am not apprentice driver again, everything will be awright. Everything will be awright. If the trouble no become fight. If the trouble become fight then wetin go happen?

I cannot answer that question. I just think of Agnes and the J.J.C.

I see Agnes again for morning time and for night – several days. Our motor still dey workshop. My master say it will take long time before the motor will commot. 'E say I fit go home go wait until the motor don ready. When I see Agnes and tell her so, she say she will follow me to Dukana. I take am reach Dukana. Her mother was very very happy to see her. All the town people too. They were saying what a fine baby Agnes is now. Everybody say she is clever girl.

I am very proud because I am the only boy that Agnes talks to every time. I think that one day I will marry Agnes.

I think so because, although she have not told me that she will marry me, I used to see how she looks at me. Then she will tell me that I am very fine man with plenty of hair for my chest and I am smiling very well all the time. She will tell me that she like as I was dancing that night in African Upwine Bar in Diobu, New York. Then some times she will say that I am very foolish man. That why I do not go to school only to be apprentice driver? And then that anyway, she does not mind that driver work because, after all said and done, the most important is for man to like his wife, take very good care of her, help her every time and to know what woman like.

So Agnes say that she likes as I used to be respecting her and how I am helping her every time. And when she is saying all this, I will just be prouding. You know, because it is good when fine girl like Agnes with J.J.C. is telling you that you are fine man. And true true I know that I am very fine boy. All the women in this Dukana used to tell me so every time. So it was not a great surprisation to me when Agnes told me that yes, she likes me.

And when I see as she was liking me quick quick I know that if I ask her to be my wife, she must say yes. However, you know as Lagos girl concern, she must want plenty money and other good things because, after all said and done, no be fine that woman will chop. As they used to sing for grammaphone, 'no money, woman no go follow you, even if you fine fine pass everybody'.

So I used to confuse when I think that one day, Agnes will be my wife. Anyway, I cannot think of that now. The most important is that I am the only boy that Agnes talks to every time. It is a sign of good omen.

LOMBER THREE

By this time Chief Birabee have finished collecting the money from the men and women. Those who cannot pay the money he takes their pot or their paddle. Everybody is cursing Chief Birabee and the government. But Chief Birabee cannot mind. And government too is far away and will not hear. Chief Birabee say that after some time the people will forget what he have done as they use to forget before. And true, after some time the people begin to forget.

As I do not travel to Pitakwa again, no plenty news of trouble again. Many people in Dukana cannot care less sef. They continue to dance and happy. Myself too I was very very happy. Because Agnes is with me. And true true she is good girl. Very clever. She knows so many things. And she is beautiful. Everyone was saying she will make good wife. And good wife for me too because she can take good care of me as she used to take good care of her master in Lagos.

But as you know, you cannot walk with girl in Dukana without people talking about it. Even sef if you want to do it, they will call you useless young man. And they will say the girl is *ashewo*, no shame. So we cannot walk about as we fit do in Diobu, New York. Even, it is like say she is different porson from the girl that I meet before in the African Upwine Bar for Diobu. But we were having jolly time. Dukana quiet as before.

But after some time now, no salt. What does this mean? One cup of salt which was costing two pence before begin to cost one shilling. I do not like it. Many people do not like it. Because our people say suffer suffer chop beans without salt. Which means that it is only proper poor man, sufferman, that will not fit buy salt put for him chop. So now that salt is costing one shilling instead of two pence for cup, it means that poor man cannot chop again. Country don spoil.

All the people were angry with Chief Birabee. They say he took money from all the people make rich man and now common salt have become rich man chop. Not nonsense be that? How Dukana man or woman go manage? If salt cost one shilling, how much cloth go cost?

I met Duzia, Bom and Kole one day in our village square. They were sitting down talking together. Duzia's work in Dukana is to talk and knack tory. Wherever you see him, he must be talking or making others to talk and they will all be laughing together. When Duzia begins to laugh even if you do not want to laugh you must laugh too. Duzia is popular man in Dukana. Very popular at all. That cripple man. Also Bom. Bom is another kain man in Dukana. He have no farm, no hoe, no canoe, no net. Every time you will see him in fishing village knacking tory. Making all the people to laugh. And they will give him all the chop he wants. Bom does not work. Any time porson die, Bom must be there. To dig the grave and talk and listen to what other people are saying. He knows everything that is happening throughout Dukana and throughout the world from Dukana to Bori. Himself and Duzia are very good friend. Very good.

Kole is old man. Very old man. Very gentle too. He cannot harm anybody. When you see him you will like him immediately. Because he is very good man. He cannot quarrel anybody. He does not talk plenty. Bom and Duzia dey respect am plenty. Because he get plenty children and plenty farm plus canoes for fishing. Even his wives are traders too. Kole get plenty money. He have built a house with zinc. And he put cement for the floor. But although, he does not proud at all. He will still talk with everybody in Dukana, chief or no chief. Rich man and poor man. Even he likes Bom and Duzia more than. Na him dey give dem chop any time they are hungry. And Kole knows everything that happened in Dukana even sixty years before. I tell you, Kole is clever man. Anything he sees he cannot forget.

And he is not like old man sef. If you see him you cannot believe that he is old man. Dukana people say it is so because every year Kole must change his blood by marrying new and young wife. Kole have plenty wife and plenty children. He is very very happy man.

So I met them as they were talking in the square. They were sitting on top of some trees on the ground talking small small. They were not happy at all. This is what they were talking as I hear 'am:

"Bom, I think it is time for us to die," said Duzia.

"Why?" Bom asked.

"Buy one cup of salt for one shilling? Whasmatter?"

"It is very worse at all. How will porson begin to buy one cup of salt for one shilling?"

"Can porson marry or even chop if salt begin to cost money like that? . . . But why? Eh? Kole. Have you seen anything like this before?" Duzia was asking.

"In all my life this is the second time that this thing have happened." Kole said. "The first time na Hitla do am. Hitla very strong man, oh. If as he is fighting, they cut off his arm today, he must return tomorrow with another hand complete and new. Very tough man at all. He first hold up all ship bringing salt to Egwanga. No salt again. Everywhere. Man picken begin to suffer. Even by that time you cannot find salt to buy at all. Now again no salt for second time. Praps some strong men have hold up all the ships again. Isn't it so, Mene?"

"I don't know," is what I answered. "How can I know?"

"But you travel every time to Pitakwa. Is it not there that the ships are stopping? Do you see ship when you go to Pitakwa?"

"Oh yes. I see ship. Plenty ship," I answered.

"Then why no salt?" Duzia asked.

"Praps na Chief Birabee dey hide all the salt. You know the man is useless man. Even if government give him the salt to give people of Dukana he must keep everything in his house. Begin to sell small small," Bom said.

"Oh yes," Duzia agreed. "Even all the money he is collecting from woman and man I think he has chopped it by himself."

"Did you pay the money?"

"How can? I no get the one for use buy chop sef, how can I buy chop for another man. Or even for government. Which kain government go begin beg poor man for money? Is that better government, Kole?"

"At all. But not government want that money. It is Chief Birabee. I know. Sometime he will send a little to government because he wants to hear his name in the radio. But only a little."

"His name in radio! Are they calling Chief Birabee's name in the radio?"

"Yes," Kole said.

"Ah – ah. This Chief Birabee is strong man after all, oh. To hear the name of our own Chief in the radio is not small thing at all. This Dukana will be important place in the world after all."

Duzia was very happy. Bom too. Even Kole begin to smile small small.

"Chief Birabee can tief any money he likes. If he can make Dukana name to get inside radio he is very good chief for me. Believe me," Bom said.

"But if he can make our name appear in the radio, why can't he tell government to send us salt so that we can eat and be happy? Even sef why no salt?"

"True, I don't know at all. This thing is beginning to confuse me small. Praps we can ask Zaza. He fit to know." That is what Kole answered at the end.

Zaza was just coming in. Zaza is very short man. The shortest man in Dukana. And very black too. Black than charcoal sef. And he does not like to wear shirt. Never. Or shoe. Every time you will see him without shirt and tying one big cloth on his waist, holding the cloth with his left hand and walking slowly slowly on the road, from his house to his mama house. Because Zaza does not cook in his own house. Zaza have no wife, nothing at all. Even he does not like to work. Every time you will see him walking, with his fat belly and plenty of hair for his chest as he does not wear shirt and walking along the road. He used to cut his hair well well and his teeth will be shining, and he must bathe well and put better oil and scent on his body. Walking to his mama's house. Na him mama dey give am chop. And Zaza will be very happy, prouding everywhere in Dukana.

Because Zaza get very powerful and beautiful voice. When you hear Zaza talking, you can know that Zaza is talking. Because it is like fine song. I am telling you. The girls in this Dukana used to like Zaza because he is fine and get beautiful hair and fine face and smile. Zaza is even very proud of everything plus the work he cannot work.

So Zaza was just coming in. He was smiling. Without shirt and no shoe. And his left hand holding his loin cloth. He entered and greeted everybody.

"Duzia, how now? Bom. Terr Kole. How is the world?" Zaza said as he entered.

"The world don spoil," Duzia said.

He made one kain sound in his mouth.

"Why? Whasmatter?" Zaza asked.

"Don't you see the world will soon end?" Bom said.

"That is what that man Pastor Barika is telling all the church people every time," Zaza said. "But I cannot believe it at all. Old soza like myself cannot believe the world will soon end because I no get salt to take chop. Why, is this the first time? Kole, I think you can remember. That time of Hitla. There was no salt in Dukana. At all. Not just one cup for one shilling. But no salt at all. People begin to use salt water to make soup. Even to get small salt which they can sell sef. Bom, Duzia, you people were here, not so? Ehen. Na only Mene be small picken by that time. Well, by that time, I no get time to stay here and begin to ask why no salt or why salt is costing too much money? Not me. I cannot waste my time like that. I just ask them why no salt? And they talk that Hitla is the man who is stopping the salt from reaching Dukana. I said this Hitla must be nonsense foolish man otherwise why will he stop salt from reaching Dukana? Does he want everybody to die? Well, I cannot allow my people in Dukana to die. So I said I must join army because I do not want my people to die. Kole, I think you remember?"

"Oh yes. I remember well well," Kole answered.

"Well, so I just went to Egwanga. I tell them I will join army one time. I am telling you, they cannot believe me when I say I will join army. Even the white man who was D.O. begin to laugh small small. How can man like me join army is what he was asking. Army is for tall tall men. Not short man. This kind of talk can vex me, you know. I look the D.O. well well. Then I tell am say no be tallness go fight the war. Na according to as how porson get strong heart. I tell the D.O. that tall or no tall I want to be soza and I will be soza whether he like it or not at all. So the D.O. ask me why I want to be soza. So I tell him it is because that man Hitla is stopping salt from reaching my people in Dukana and I cannot allow that type of thing otherwise all my people will die because of no salt which will be big shame for ever because to die because of no salt mean that porson is very very poor and it is big shame to be poor. So the D.O. began to laugh small small. Then he look at me for long time. Me I look am well too, straight for him face. I no fear. I no shame. Haba. Zaza, you are good man before."

Zaza was looking at me, prouding as he was talking.

"White man begin to laugh for himself again, small small. I think he begin to like me. But me I cannot like his long nose. 'Awright. I will allow you to become soza. Yes. I will make you soza,' he begin to talk with him long nose. 'I will make you soza'.

"I tell you I was very very happy when the man begin to talk like that. I know I will get all the thing I want. And believe me, I was now thinking of how I will hold Hitla and bring him to Dukana in a bag of salt so that people will cut him and put him inside soup and eat his meat with salt. Even sef I was prouding plenty. When they gave me the uniform with big black boot and hat, I wear am return to Dukana for just one day. It was by that time that plenty young boys saw me and they begin to say they will join army too.

"When I returned to Egwanga there was plenty of work. Very soon they were saying that we will travel to oversea to fight. I tell you I was prouding plenty. Because it is in oversea that I can catch Hitla. And it is in oversea that I will find woman to marry, especially as I hear that woman does not cost money there. Even sef, if porson want to marry na the woman go give am all the money. Woman plus him family. So I was prouding and telling all my friends that now everything will be awright. So I ask one my friend to write me letter which I will send to my mother. I want to tell her not to worry whether him see me or not because I must return whether whether. Then that my friend write the letter and I post am. I was prouding of myself.

"The next day now they put us inside ship. Look ehn, I have not seen that kind of thing before. Plenty of us inside one ship and the ship was dancing in the ocean, left right, left left right. Quick slow, quick quick slow. And the belly of many of those sozas was turning, slow, quick quick slow, quick. They were vomitting like no man business. Haba. But not myself, man picken! Not at all. I am telling you.

"Two weeks like that, then we stop. By that time all those sozas done become like woman. If no be for man like myself I think we all for don shame. But when they see me, they were all prouding because the officers were saying what fine man I am, what fine man I am. And myself I was prouding because they were saying what fine man I am. I know that I will bring back Hitla and the salt to Dukana."

You can see that Zaza is enjoying himself plenty as he is talking. Looking at Duzia, Bom and Terr Kole as if to say 'I think you see that I am tough man'. Then he continued:

"So now we all came down from that ship. Everything in that place was new for we eye. I never see beautiful place like that town, I am telling you. Tall tall building. Long long motor. White people. Everything. Them call the place Burma. Oh, Burma, I cannot forget Burma. But not the white people, tall building and long long motor interest me. At all at all. I am looking for Hitla everywhere. I said to myself, where is this foolish man who have make it difficult to chop in Dukana? Where is this foolish man who is holding all ships and cannot allow ship to come to Dukana? I want to see him. I want to hold am, I want to tell am that he is very very very stupid man and then I will beat 'im helele. That is what I was telling myself. Then they put us in lorry to take us away to another place. Already, we were all very hungry. Many people in that lorry were crying because of no chop. But not myself. I was thinking of how I will return to Dukana with the head of that Hitla. Then everybody will come out of the house and they will be shouting, 'Zaza! Zaza! Welcome, Zaza, our son, our brave son.' And how I will be prouding like man who just marry young beautiful wife.

"The lorry was moving very fast and after some time I

cannot see anything again. Only all those people in the lorry who were crying and crying because of no chop. I no worry. But this no chop na waya oh.

"After some time now the lorry stopped. Then we all came down. Then they begin to divide us again. Some people will travel again, that is what they said. All those boys wey come from Egwanga with me were no longer with me. As they were going away, they were shouting to me. They were crying and saying 'Goodbye, Zaza', 'Goodbye, Zaza'. I was smiling and prouding. It was very wonderful thing. Forest everywhere. And Hitla plenty for that forest. You kill Hitla today, tomorrow one hundred Hitla appear. You cut him leg today, tomorrow he get twenty legs. Haba. Hitla na strong man, I am telling you. But na we strong pass am. Gun sef they no give we. Na when they think say Hitla dey hide for one corner of the forest that they will send us to see whether Hitla is there at all. Then we will begin to walk small small with our belly to that part of the forest. No gun in our hand oh. Only the white people get gun and they were behind us. Na we only go fit catch Hitla with our hand. Without gun the white people no fit fight. Because Hitla is their brother and him get gun, they must fight him with gun. But we cannot get gun because Hitla no be we brother. So we will go slowly to the place where Hitla is. But Hitla cannot be seen in the forest. Because Hitla is very clever man. If you look for him on the ground, na lie. Hitla is not on the ground. He is on top of tree like monkey. Na on top of the tree that Hitla is staying and sleeping. Na there Hitla dey cook and chop. So if you want Hitla you must look on top of the tree. Then if so therefore you begin to look on top of the tree only, you will not find Hitla at all. Because now he is not on top of the tree. He have big big hole in the ground like rabbit, and he is sleeping there like rabbit too. It is inside this hole that he is cooking and chopping and shitting. Even he is sleeping and bathing there. It is his house. Every white man was calling him bastard. We too call him bastard. I don't know what he was calling us. Every day we were fighting and cutting him but still he will come again. The more we kill him the more he comes. Praps that is why they call him bastard. We were fighting and cutting him for two years and then he will still come again after we have killed him.

"I am telling you this thing wondered me plenty. How can you fight porson, kill him and then the porson will return again? If you kill him twenty times he will return twenty one times. If you cut his hand, his hand will appear again tomorrow. God in Heaven. So, however, we were fighting and fighting. With gun, without gun. Some time, as I have said before, no food, some time, no water. Even sef you have to put your urine inside water bottle and after some time you will drink the urine because of no water. *Tufia*! What man picken have seen only God can know."

Then Zaza stopped talking and looked at all of us as we were listening to him. Bom's mouth was open, listening. Zaza began to smile.

"I am telling all you useless people, useless young man in Dukana walking about with small loin cloth talking nonsense and fighting with your mother because she have not prepared chop for you in time, I am telling you that you are all very very stupid because you do not know that life is very hard and young man must struggle hard if he will succeed in life."

I know that Zaza is saying this one now because of myself, Mene. As he is saying it, he is looking at me. He cannot talk like that to Kole and Bom and Duzia because they old pass am. But he can speak to me anyhow and tell me that I am very very stupid. Myself, very very stupid? Nonsense. Even sef, this Zaza is not better man. He have no work and no wife. No shoe and no shirt. He cannot be prouding for man like myself who is apprentice driver. Is it because he have fine voice and he cut his hair fine and he put fine scent and that type of thing? Is that why he can call me very very stupid? Even sef the man is chopping from his mother's kitchen like all those young men he is talking about. Is it because he have fought in the war before? Praps. Or he think that other people cannot fight?

Even, as I see how Kole and Duzia and Bom are respecting this man, allowing him to talk and they cannot talk even one word to him, just listening to him with their mouth open like *mumu*, respecting Zaza with his fat belly, I am telling you I was very angry. Very very angry. I think I begin to jealous the man small. Small small. As I was thinking all this one for myself in my mind, Zaza have begun to speak again.

"So everyday I fight this Hitla man. Without stop. Others were lying there with gun and those without gun. But not Zaza from Dukana. I fight for three years in the forest of Burma. Haba. You can hear the gun in the night making *Gbagam! Gbaga gbaga gbagam!! Kijijim!! Kikijijigim!* As gun sound na so man dey die. Man picken wey him mama happy when dem born am. Even after some time, Hitla begin to bring aeroplane. And if you see how that aeroplane was shitting proper bomb, heavy heavy bomb, I am telling you, you will surprise plenty. As the aeroplane shit, na so porson dey die. Forest dey burn, ground dey spoil.

"But myself, I cannot die. I know that I must conquer Hitla. That I must bring his head to Dukana. That I will not allow him to stop my mother from eating salt. That after I have conquered him then I will marry his sister and bring her to Dukana as my wife. And then the people of Dukana will see that I am their own son and they will be prouding of me as I will be prouding of myself.

"For all that time that we were in Burma, each time that Hitla see me, he will begin to run and hide. He have gun, myself no gun. Still he will be hiding. On top of tree like monkey. Behind bush like bad spirit. Inside hole like rabbit. Shitting and eating and sleeping, even dying inside hole. Sometimes when I go to look for him he have just run from the hole leaving all his thing there. Book and pen and everything. Even when Hitla is fighting he is also reading and writing. Writing plenty. This man sef! The day I will catch am ehn, 'e go shit for him trouser. So I continued to pursue him from corner to corner. Wherever they talk that Hitla dey, na there Zaza will go.

"All this time I was thinking of Dukana. How are my people now? Are they thinking of me? Are they chopping well now? All this one I am fighting Hitla, can Hitla still stop ship that is bringing salt to Dukana? Do those my people in Dukana know that myself Zaza and all these white people we are fighting Hitla so that salt will reach Dukana? I don't think they know. Because if they know they will be praying for me. Some time they are praying and I do not know. Praps that is why they have not killed me yet. If people in Dukana were not praying for me some time Hitla will have kill me already. So I continue to turn this thing for my mind. And when I think how all the people will gratulate me when the war don finish and Hitla done die, I begin to proud of myself small small again.

"But suppose I die sef, what will happen? Will they take my body to Dukana so that they can bury me well? Nonsense. How can brave man like myself die? Brave man cannot die in war. Only all these stupid people wey dey fear, dey shit in their trousers. Useless people. Only them fit die in war. So I must capture Hitla. I tell you, I fight am like lion with wound. And everybody was respecting me.

"After some time, they said that I have fought very well and they asked me to go on leave. Leave? Will I go back to Dukana when I have not yet catch Hitla? I am telling you, this leave did not please me at all. So I tell them I cannot go. Then our big man called me. He say, 'Look my friend. All this *kaji jim*, *kaji jim* that you are hearing here can make you deaf. All this running that you are running here can make you lame. All this hunting that you are hunting here can kill you. And all this starving that you are starving can make you to die. And if you die do you think you can help us to kill Hitla? Instead, Hitla will kill you first because he is a very strong man. So therefore do not say that you will not go on leave. Go on leave and stay there for two weeks. Then you can return again and begin to look for Hitla. Some time during your leave, you can find one nice girl who will make you happy.' That is what our big man said.

"Even sef there was plenty sense in everything he said. Plenty sense. When I turned the thing for my mind, I know that there is plenty sense in what he said. I come happy. Even what made me happy pass is that one about nice girl who will make me happy. It is by that time that I begin to remember that I have not married and even I have not sleep with woman since I came to this Burma. So I do not please with myself again. Which kain war that will stop a man from sleeping with woman? Is it not during war that somebody will sleep with plenty women? Especially brave man like myself?

"That is why I went on leave. And lo and behold, no sooner I get to the town than I find wife to marry. Ha! Zaza, son of Mina, God don butter your bread. Zaza, child of Dukana, your strong head don bring you better. Marry wife without money.

Ha! ha! I was laughing and prouding and enjoying my life with my new wife. Oh, it was jolly jolly. Zaza! You na man!"

As Zaza was knacking this tory you can see that he was enjoying himself proper. He was looking at Terr Kole and Duzia and Bom. And he saw that they were happy and prouding of him as Dukana man. Because in Dukana if your son goes out and brings something good, then you will begin to proud because he have made your name to go far place. As Zaza is son of Dukana, every Dukana man must to be proud because Zaza have married woman from far country before before. Zaza was looking at me now to see whether I myself will be prouding because of him. But I don't think I was prouding plenty. So he put his hand inside the fold of his loin cloth and bring out one foto. Then he showed me the foto.

God in Heaven! This Zaza is not very useless man after all, you know. Look at him sitting inside the foto wearing long trouser and coat and his hand passing round the neck of one beautiful white woman who wear better dress and shoe and who was smiling and looking at Zaza as Zaza was looking at her straight for him eyes. Chei, this Zaza man na *waya* oh. Na *waya* oh.

Zaza was looking at me as I was looking at the foto. He was prouding when he saw as I was looking. Before I can open my mouth, Zaza have begun to answer the very question wey I bin wan ask am.

"Oh yes, I fuck am well well."

Terr Kole, Duzia and Bom begin to laugh. But na Duzia laugh pass all the others. Duzia was laughing with his body shaking. He was shouting 'fuck, fuck, fuck, fuck' and laughing, rolling on the ground. 'Zaza you fucking dog, God punish you', he said.

"I agree," Bom replied, laughing.

Zaza was laughing too, small small.

"Oh yes, I fuck am to nonsense. Not two weeks I spend there. Two months. Three months. The woman no gree me go. She say I am the best fucker in the world. From soza to fucker. Like everything I want to do I must do it well well. That is my life. Anyway, after some time I have to return to look for Hitla. I get am, and I kill am. But when I return to look for my wife, she have died. Only the foto of her that I get. That is why I cannot marry any woman again. I cannot forget that my first wife. I cannot at all, I am telling you."

"But why did you not bring one long hair from that woman's yarse?" Duzia asked.

Zaza begin to laugh small, smiling big and laughing. Zaza was prouding plenty. He shake his head like to say: 'This Duzia, you are stupid man. Talking useless things every time.' Zaza did not answer the question that Duzia asked.

It was Terr Kole who spoke next. He said:

"Now, Zaza, I hear another war have started. Are you going to fight again?"

"Me? Fight again?" Zaza begin to laugh one small laugh from him belly. "No, Terr Kole. I will not fight again. I have fought the important fight before. I cannot fight again. Even this war you are hearing about now is like children playing. They don't have better gun, nothing. And no woman to marry sef. Let the young people like Mene here go and fight. I cannot fight again. I have killed my own Hitla. Let Mene them go and fight."

"Yes," said Duzia," the young men should go and fight now. It is their time."

"Mene, I think you hear what these men are saying?" Bom asked me.

"Oh yes. I am sure he have heard you", replied Terr Kole. And after that, I said goodbye to them and went away.

As I was walking away that evening, I was thinking plenty of things. How Zaza was prouding in Dukana, carrying picture of fine woman, in his loin cloth. And Terr Kole, Duzia and Bom looking at him prouding as he was knacking the tory of all the things he did at Burma. But can all those things be true? Sometimes. Then I remembered as he was saying 'I have killed my own Hitla. Let Mene them go and fight.' And then I remember what Agnes told me for the African Upwine Bar: 'when trouble come, I like strong, brave man who can fight and defend me!'

So all these things were turning in my head, turning, turning as I was walking away, slowly slowly leaving Terr Kole, Terr Zaza, Duzia and Bom in the playground. I begin to confuse. I remember that tall man and the short man who were chopping *ngwongwo* in the African Upwine Bar at Diobu. The tall man was saying 'it is good thing to fight. If somebody take your thing byforce, if 'e want byforce you to do something wey you no like to do, then you fit fight am.' All these things can confuse porson.

And as I am walking to see Agnes, I begin to glad. I think it is good thing to fight after all. If porson will marry better woman after the fight. Oh yes, it must be good thing to fight. And not just fight with hand and leg oh, but better fight with gun. And not just for Dukana but for Burma.

By the time I get to the house of Agnes him mama, my brain don begin clear small small. I was glad by now. Even, when I think that I will see Agnes again I begin to glad more than. My man begin to stand up like snake wey no get house.

LOMBER FOUR

It was beautiful new moon for Dukana. You can see all the plantain and banana as they are standing straight and tall inside the moon. No wind at all. And the people are beating drum and dancing in another part of the town. True, true, these Dukana people no get sense at all. How can they be dancing, singing and jollying when there is trouble for the country? If they no take time something will happen for this town and when that thing will happen it is because they cannot think as other people are thinking. In Pitakwa and Diobu New York, everybody is talking about the trouble, preparing about the trouble, making money whether na transport or trade. But in Dukana Pastor Barika is saying the world will soon end. And Chief Birabee is only chopping money from people, no plan. And Zaza is going about, no shoe and big loin cloth for him waist and no shirt with foto of white woman prouding and insulting young men. I think to myself, if trouble begin proper, Dukana go see pepper.

Agnes sweet like tomato. I am telling you. If Agnes was not living in Dukana, I will have gone to Pitakwa to look at the motor since. But because she is in Dukana, I must stay here so I can be able to see her always. And I see her plenty. In the morning, in the afternoon and for night. I must always pass in front of their house. And when I am passing there I must talk loud or laugh plenty or make any type of noise which will make her know that I am passing. And sometimes she will appear and greet me. Sometimes I will see her as she is working or hear her as she is singing. And I will say to myself 'Chei! this girl fine oh'. In short, I like the girl very much and I will like her to be my wife. I don't think I can return to Pitakwa again. Whether whether.

You know as we people in Dukana dey make our thing. If you like a girl you cannot show it to everybody openly. It is not as they used to do in the cinema, those white people, kissing every time. No. In fact, if you love a girl in Dukana then you must beat her small small. That will show that you love her. But I don't think Agnes is just like those stupid Dukana girls. Even, she can discuss anything you like. She is a clever girl. Very clever girl. I must marry her. That is what I tell myself every time.

One day, when I meet Agnes for road, I tell her that I want to marry her. She did not even reply me. Then I asked her what is the matter that she does not want to reply to my word. Then she laughed. She laughed plenty. And she said, "You foolish man. All your friends are making soza, you want to stay here and marry with that your thing standing like snake wey no get house."

Hei, this Agnes sef. What kain girl be dis? Everytime she will be talking careless talk. So I told her she doesn't know me. I am better than any soza sef, only I must first get my driving licence. She laughed again.

"Okay!" she said, "when you get your driving licence and enter the army and you begin to fight like better man wey get sense and power, then you can come back and show me that your man wey still dey stand like snake."

Then she walked away. And just look at her as she is walking. Her bottom fine oh. Just smooth like wetin call and her bobby just stand up like calabash. I will do anything so that this fine girl can be my wife and I can be sleeping with her on one bed every night.

Many many times I used to think of this two things. Number one. Zaza. That *ye-ye man*, proper *yafu yafu* man, just moving about in Dukana prouding because he fight against Hitla and abusing young people like myself that we must go and fight. Then number two. Agnes. Fine girl. Very fine girl at all. She likes strong man who will defend am if trouble come. Awright.

I will show Zaza that I am not *yekpe* man like himself. I will show that Agnes that I am not a coward man. I can defend her anytime. Oh yes. I will show her proper.

So every time I am thinking of these things. For sleep oh. For chop oh. For work or anything at all. Everyday, I must think of this war, fight, Zaza and his prouding stupidity and Agnes plus her beauty and love for me. And I come confuse proper.

So one evening, as we were playing football for the church field, we heard the sound of lorry. At first I think that it is my master's lorry that have returned from Pitakwa. Everybody was telling me: 'Ah-ha, you will now go to work again you foolish boy instead to stay here looking for woman to sleep with and playing football without work, chopping your mama chop for nothing.' Myself too I begin to glad small small. Because if I can be going to Pitakwa everyday, it means to say that when I return every night, they will begin to ask me of how the world is, what is happening whether there is fight or no fight. Then I can tell that stupid Chief Birabee what other people are doing in the world. And sometimes I can bring Agnes my dear some better thing from the shop which she will like and thank me for it. So I begin to run towards the motor. But when I get there now, soso soza soza. I am telling you when I see these sozamen inside their khaki and all of them holding gun, I was afraid small. My heart begin to cut, *gbum, gbum, gbum*. I stopped and I begin to go back small small.

Because it is not good to show that na you sabi pass especially when other people no dey show. Even sef everybody for that Dukana when they see the sozas, they begin to hide, close door. The sozas were walking, prouding, asking for the chief.

"Who is the chief of this village?"

Then I see Chief Birabee coming. There was one soza behind him. Chief Birabee no get hair for the front of him face. He begin to sweat for him bald head. He was shaking like *shege*. When they bring him before the big soza captain, he begin to smile like idiot fool, his mouth shaking. He cannot even answer the question which they are asking him.

"Are you the chief of this village?" The big soza captain was asking him.

"No, sah".

"Who is the chief of this village?"

"Na yourself sah".

"What?"

"Well, you know, sah . . . ehm . . . ehm."

"Look, do you understand English at all?"

Chief Birabee begin to shake him head. Then he called me with hand to come. To tell you the truth when I see how Chief Birabee is confusing before this man, I am very very angry. How can Dukana chief begin to fear before small soza, even if sef that sozaman is soza captain. If na Dukana man now, this Chief Birabee will be shouting and prouding and bullying on him. So when I came near him he begin to speak Kana to me. This time no fear for him voice. He is not smiling idiot fool smile. He is giving order.

"Ehm, tell everybody to bring out all the goats, chicken and plantain they have. We must give it to these big sozas, my friends who have been sent by the government to come and see how we are getting on here in Dukana. Do you hear me? Get moving. Tell everyone what I have said."

Look ehn, this thing surprised me *helele*. This is Chief Birabee who is fearing for the soza, but giving me order in big strong voice. What does that mean? And when I look at the soza captain sef, it is not that he is big or anything. He is not bigger than myself. I am sure that if it come to fight, I can fight him well well, gun or no gun. I am still turning this thing for my mind when, lo and behold, like magic, all the big big men in Dukana begin to bring goat, yam, chicken and plantain. They full the motor of the soza people. Even one man bring him daughter to give the soza captain. But the sozaman do not want the girl so she went away crying.

Then the soza captain entered into his lorry and they drive away, himself and his other sozamen. They were waving goodbye and smiling and laughing happily. Chief Birabee was waving more than sef. Afterwards he begin to boast and proud to the people.

"I am friend of the government now, you see. You stupid people of Dukana. When I tell you to do what I say, you cannot understand. Do you see now? Government have sent soza here to come and see you people, protect you people, love your sons and your daughters. All because Chief Birabee is here. You see now?"

The people were talking about it that night. In this Dukana, everything is completely different. By the time people were talking about it, you will think that God have visited Dukana. Even Agnes begin to ask me whether I see the fine fine sozas wey come to Dukana. I told her that I did not see any fine fine soza, only they are wearing khaki wey dey never wash since long time. She begin to laugh and say that I am common civilian, I cannot understand like brave sozaman.

Well, all these things begin to confuse me. So everybody like those sozamen who come to Dukana ehn? So they like as Chief Birabee was smiling idiot smile, giving all the chop in Dukana to those sozas? So that is what Dukana like ehn, including my dear Agnes? Praps na me one be the fool for the town. Because all these things are vexing me. Praps na me one be fool proper.

I can think something in my mind for a long time. Throughout that week, that is what I was doing. Turning that visit of sozamen for my mind. And I have plenty to think about oh. Because from that time more and more sozas begin to come to Dukana. Every time when they come they will cut all the plantain plus banana. Some time sef they will enter porson house begin to ask for chop. And if the porson do not give them chop, they will hala and hala and then begin to beat the women. Then afterwards they begin to make debt collector in Dukana. If I owe you money and I cannot pay, then you will call soza for me. The soza will come and begin to bully on me until I give you the money. Then you and the sozaman will share the money. But if after he have bullied on me I still cannot pay, then they will beat me proper proper till blood commot from my mouth and body and they will take me away to the soza people camp and prison me there. One time they beat Zaza proper proper. By that time Zaza does not know what to do. He forget sef that he is old soza before. He forget the foto of his woman from Burma. If you see Zaza by then you will sorry for him. He does not even know why they are beating him.

But even although these things were happening, the Dukana people cannot complain at all. Chief Birabee is still smiling his idiot smile always and when any sozas come it is to his house they will first go. Then he will give them drink and chop. Chief Birabee like to do all this because when the sozas are there, he can have power more than in Dukana. By that time nobody can disobey what him talk like before. Yes, because before before, this Chief Birabee is chief but he is not very important. He cannot prison anybody and if you like, you can refuse to go and judge your case in his house. After all he have no police or kotuma, so if you disobey him what can he do to you? Chief is no chief nowadays. Only to tief, chopping money from poor woman plus money wey dem collect for village.

So as I was saying, all the people in Dukana were less concerned with what was happening. I by myself I was very very angry, because, as you know, no young man will like to stay for his hometown and see how they are using his people like cow, goat or okro soup. Worst of all myself.

I was thinking that I am the only man who is not happy with these soza boys. Not so oh. There is one thick man in this Dukana. Young man oh, but thick like sandpaper. Everybody say he is lawyer but no be so. Everybody think he is small boy but na lie. He knows something. I am telling you. Since all this wahala begin this thick man just dey stay inside his house like snail. Very very quiet. Every time that you will pass near his house he is listening to radio or writing. Ha, what kind of man is this? Ehn? Can't he go out or talk with somebody? And why always listening to radio? And he is Dukana man, oh. Why can't he talk with our people. Why can't he talk with Chief Birabee and the rest chiefs?

Then one Sunday, this thick man wey no dey go to church sef begin go church. I see am that day as he was entering our church. What does he want? Throughout that church, I was looking at the thick man. And this thick man was singing well well and in Kana too. This type of thing wonder me oh. Even I cannot care for all the things that are happening in that church. Every time I am looking at the thick man. Then the thick man begin to walk to the pulpit. Everywhere was very quiet. What is the thick man going to say? Will he speak English and use terprita or will he speak Kana? So I was thinking all these things when the man begin to pray. Everybody said Amen and then they sat down. Waiting. To hear. What the thick man will say.

This thick man wey no dey go church. But who have come to church today.

As you know, when catechist stands up to preach in pulpit, this thing can never end. He will be shouting, abusing woman who goes to another man, he will be saying anything that comes to his head. He can amuse the people too, oh. But today, the thick man is very serious. He just take one line from the Bible. 'You people are the salt in the soup.' Salt in the soup! Have you heard anything like this before? Porson is salt in the soup? I begin to turn this thing for my mind and after some time I begin to understand. Because if salt is not inside soup, then it cannot be soup at all. Nobody can fit to chop it. Therefore, that salt is very important to everyone. To the soup and to the people who will chop the soup too. Then the thick man asked: 'Suppose that salt no get salt inside it, what will happen?' This kain question na war oh. How can salt not get salt inside it. Ehn? How can salt not get salt inside? Will it be salt? It cannot be salt. Oh yes, it cannot be salt. That is what the man was saying. I 'gree with am. Awright, if na we be the salt, and we no get salt inside our salt wey be ourselves, can we be ourselves? Wait oh. Wait oh. Wait small. Make I no too confuse. Say this thing again, thick man. Yes. If na we be the salt, and we no get salt inside our salt wey be ourselves, can we be ourselves? Look, my friend, I no dey for all dis *ugbalugba* case. Abi, dis man think that we are in University? Am I not common motor apprentice? How can I understand this salt and ourselves and no be salt and 'e be salt? Anyway, any salt wey no get salt inside no be salt and it must be thrown away. Awright, thick man. How this one concern we people for this Dukana? What he mean to say, therefore, is that any man wey no be man, he will be thrown away. He is useless man. Every man get something which his God have give him. Everyman must be brave and talk with another man. Why run away if another man, whether he holds gun or not, comes to your house? Why run away? Why smile idiot foolish smile to porson who have come to tief and give you moless? What are you fearing, you people of Dukana? Where will this fear take you to? Every time you are dancing, singing and you do not know what is happening outside, and you do not ask. All these sozas who are coming to tief and beat up people in Dukana, making debt collector, are they not men like ourselves? Why is there no Dukana boy among the sozas? Cannot our own boys join the sozas? Suppose Dukana boy is soza do you think they will beat our Zaza, that old soza, as they beat am the other day? No, you people. Don't forget that you are salt. And salt must be inside your salt otherwise they will throw you away like *mumu*, foolish idiot. Amen.

Trouble have begun again, oh. Every time I must get something to turn for my mind. What this thick man have said is very confusing. And true. Yes. Suppose Dukana man is soza will he beat Dukana people? If Dukana man is not soza I think these sozas will continue to come here to beat our people, throw them away like salt wey no get salt inside their salt? Then I add to this what Agnes my darling was saying that she like brave man who will protect her when war comes and how she was prouding when those sozas came the first time to Dukana. Then I add what Zaza was saying that day when he was talking to Terr Kole and Duzia and Bom — 'Let Mene them go and fight.' — And also I think of Zaza and his white woman in that foto and how Zaza was fighting and killing Hitla in Burma. And I think again of Agnes, my darling. I think it is good thing to go to army. To be soza. Praps.

Every day, I am turning this thing in my mind. In the morning oh, in the afternoon oh, for night. As I am sleeping. As I am chopping. Every time. I think it is good thing to go to army. And I begin to think that I must join army. Praps. Praps. But first I must continue to live in Dukana and do what all the other boys are doing. Going to be soza is not good thing. That is what the boys were saying. Because soza is stupid useless anmal who will just shoot and kill and then he can also be shoot and kill. Only stupid person who want to die quick can be soza. Na so the boys talk.

So we all continue to be playing football every afternoon. And after the football we will go and swim in the river. And then I will go and chop my mama chop. Before I sleep.

Still the lorry dey for workshop. And all the time no work for me to do. Only to sit in the village square knacking tory with Duzia, Bom, Terr Kole and others. And going message for Chief Birabee. And all the time, they are talking of fighting and war, and how the radio is saying that everybody must be ready to fight and to make war. And we must not allow any stranger that we do not know to enter our town because strangers can spoil all the things in the town and kill all of us.

And always I am thinking whether I will join the sozas and fight or I will just stay in Dukana and hear Zaza abusing me and prouding of himself as old soza from Burma war. This is what I am thinking. In the morning. In the afternoon. In the night. Even in dream.

LOMBER FIVE

So one afternoon as we were playing football one policeman came and told us that we must go to the church now now. Church from football? With sweat on our bodies? This policeman must be stupid. What is his trouble, anyway? Can policeman confuse himself like this? If it is *kotuma*, somebody will understand. Because after all, *kotuma* is just man with small education, no plenty job, just chopping small small bribe from woman or man in Dukana. But police is big man going on transfer from Lagos to Kano and so on. And he can be promoted too to sarzent, then inspector and so on. So it is not good that he should confuse himself. So, nevertheless, since he say we must go to church, we all begin to go there. Everybody. Are we going to pray in the church, and today is not Sunday? Will this police force us to begin to pray? Ha!

As we entered the church now, not only those who were playing football were inside that church. Everybody in Dukana. Plus Chief Birabee, smiling that idiot foolish smile which he will be smiling whenever he sees soza or police or power. Trouble don come again, oh. Even people who do not go to church are entering this church today. I beg, God, make you no vex for these people, and this nonsense police who is causing all this trouble. So we waited inside the church. People were talking, talking. Because in this Dukana people will always talk. After some time, Chief Birabee with idiot smile looking at policeman begin to shout "Keep quiet all of you, oh! Keep quiet all of you, oh!" Then after some time he will shout again,

"Keep quiet all of you, oh. Hei! Why can't you people close your mouth?" The people will keep quiet for small time then after some time they will begin to hala again.

As you see these Dukana people, they are not talking anything good oh. I can see they are all fearing, because once they see police or soza or even *kotuma*, they must begin to fear. Useless people. And when they are fearing like that, they cannot say what is inside their mind. Just smiling idiot foolish smile like that Chief Birabee smile. Myself too, I was not happy as they have called us to church and leaving us there just like that. So after some time one motor begin to come. At first I think that it is my master's motor. But not so. It is small car. And the porson who is inside it come down quickly. He is wearing better cloth, so you can see at once that he is a very important porson. As he walked into the church, the police shouted "All stand". Everybody stood up. The man in fine shirt walked to where Chief Birabee was sitting and shook hand with him. Chief Birabee was smiling that his foolish idiot smile, super. Prouding. Because the man with fine shirt is shaking hand with him in front of the Dukana people.

The man with fine shirt sat down and we all sat down too. Plenty of talking.

"Silence!" shouted the police. "Silence, I say!"

The people cannot understand him. They were laughing because of how he was shouting. Myself too, I was laughing. Then the police came to where I was sitting and used his stick on my head. Everybody kept quiet. I stopped laughing by force. That is how my own things are. Every time trouble. Always. So I kept quiet with several people shouting little shouts inside my head from the policeman's stick's blow. I said to myself, 'trouble don begin'.

The man with fine shirt stood up. And begin to talk in English. Fine fine English. Big big words. Grammar. 'Fantastic. Overwhelming. Generally. In particular and in general'. Haba, God no go vex. But he did not stop there. The big grammar continued. 'Odious. Destruction. Fighting'. I understand that one. 'Henceforth. General mobilisation. All citizens. Able-bodied. Join the military. His Excellency. Powers conferred on us. Volunteers. Conscription'. Big big words. Long long grammar. 'Ten heads. Vandals. Enemy.' Everybody was silent. Everywhere was silent like burial ground. Then they begin to interpret all that long grammar plus big big words in Kana. In short what the man is saying is that all those who can fight will join army.

My heart begin to cut. Plenty. Join army? For what? So I am now a soza. No. No. I cannot be soza. Soza for what? Ehn? I begin to shout, No. No. The man with fine shirt was looking at me. The policeman was coming to me. Is he coming to take me to be soza? The policeman was coming. My heart was cutting, beating like drum. *Tam tum. Tam tum tum.* Then I see that it is not just one policeman but many sozas. Plenty of them with gun pointing at me. My heart was beating. *Tam tum, tam tum tum.* I don't want to be soza. So as I see them coming with their gun, I jumped out of that church and started to run. Then I heard Chief Birabee and the others shouting "Hold am! hold am!" They were shouting from every side. Then the sozas started running after me. Pursuing me. I ran and ran like a dog. Still the sozas pursued me, pointing their gun.

Oh my father wey don die, help me today. Put power inside my body. Make I no tire. I can hear the sozas saying "You are now a soza. You will fight the enemy." Na lie. Na lie. I ran towards the river. The sozas and the police were still following me. Then when I got to the river, I just jumped inside it and begin to swim. All those sozas cannot catch me. They cannot swim like myself. They are afraid of the river.

Then when I reached the other side of the river, I stopped. I went out of the water. My khaki was wet. I sat down on the white sand. No sooner than one thousand sozas appeared behind me, all their guns pointing at my back. God in Heaven. What kain trouble be dis? Immediately I jumped into the river again and begin to swim to the other side. My heart begin to beat drum more than before. *Tam tum tum. Tam tum tum. Tam tum tum.* I was swimming. I am afraid of the sozas. I do not want to join the sozas. Now the sozas do not follow me, they begin to shoot their guns: *Tako, tako. Tako – tako – tako.* Oh, Jesus. You know, I am young boy. I have never do anybody any bad thing since they born me. You know I love my neighbour as myself. Even I am good Samaritan several times. I have not called another man's wife. I have not tief another person money. I do not go juju house. Forgive me my tresspasses. *Tako, tako, tako.* My heart was beating, *tam tum tum. Tam tum tum.* I have not tief another person money. *Toko, tako, tako.* Oh my mother, pray for me, make these sozas no kill me. Let them kill snake, leopard and tiger. All those bad animals who live inside bush. But make them no kill me.

I was swimming all this time, oh. Then I reach the other bank again and I climbed it and got into the bush. The bush catch my leg and wound me for body. My body all full of wound. Blood. The blood of our Lord Jesus Christ. Oh God, help me, I beg you in the name of Jesus. I will do everything you want. I will be good boy from now till kingdom come. The sozas were still following me. Shooting. And I was running like dog.

I run until I get back to the church in Dukana. Now nobody in the church at all. All those people who were there are not there again. Now I look through the window of the church and I see all the sozas, very many of them moving like forest towards the church. They were not shooting again. They were singing very loud:

> My father don't you worry
> My mother don't you worry
> If I happen to die in the battle field
> Never mind we shall meet again.

Fear catch me well well as the sozas are moving towards the church. So I ran. From the church. I ran to my mama's house where I used to stay. But when I got there, my mama's house is not standing again. Ah – ah. Where is my mama house? Where have it disappeared to? What have happened to it? And where is my mama?

Then the sozamen began to sing another song:

> Why do you delay
> Come and save the nation
> Why do you delay
> Come and save the nation
> Oh why do you delay
> Come and save the nation

There is danger
Why do you delay?

So now when I hear there is danger my mind come go to Agnes.
I am thinking what has happened to her. So I come run to her
house. And when I get there I see that her house is not there too.
And she is not here either. So what have happened to Agnes and
her mama? Oh God, what is happening?

Then the sozas began to sing another song:

We are sozas marching for our nation
In the name of Jesus we shall conquer.

The sozas were moving nearer now. And then they begin to
shoot. *Tako, tako, tako.* And still I cannot see Agnes. And I do not
see my mama too. And my mama house and Agnes mama house
are not there. And all the Dukana people have disappeared. Not
even one person in the town. Fear cut my heart. The sozas were
moving nearer and their bullet begin to fall near me. Plenty
bullets. I begin to shout "Mama, mama, mama!" I was shouting
like that when I opened my eyes.

Ah, so it is all dream. Very bad dream. Already, day don
begin to break. My mama come to ask me why I am calling her.
I told her that I was dreaming. I told my mama how I dream of
many many sozas singing song and shooting gun and pursuing
me. And I ran away from them and fell into the river and how
they continued to pursue me. And how I return to Dukana and I
cannot find her or her house. And all the people of Dukana are
no longer there.

My mama told me that she too have been dreaming how
aeroplane came to Dukana and dropped big big mortars on top
of the church and how everybody was afraid and running about
and hiding and calling God to help them. And she ran with them
but I was not near her and she started looking for me but she
could not find me.

Well, well, well, this dream and my own are almost
identical. What can it mean? I tell you, I was very confused that
morning. And that day I was turning the dreams for my mind.
And I remembered too what the tall man said at the Upwine
Bar. What Agnes said. What Zaza said. What the thick man

said about salt and no salt inside the salt of our body. I fear.

And now everyday they were talking more and more about the war. The radio was shouting about it all the time. And they were saying that everybody must be ready for it. Trouble!

LOMBER SIX

T hen one morning, the D.O. came to Dukana. This thing was a great surprision to all of us. I think you understand. Because D.O. cannot just come to Dukana like that unless something special have happened. When he came sef, his face tight like Post Office. And he was not speaking to anybody. Only Chief Birabee. I knew that afterwards Chief Birabee will be prouding because D.O. have come to his house and is speaking to him. Anyway after some time the D.O. drove his motor away with loud noise and his face still tight. I begin to say to myself 'Trouble don begin again!'

That night the town-crier went round Dukana beating drum and saying that all young men must go to make one important meeting which they are going to make in Pitakwa. He cannot say what the meeting is for. Only that young men must go. Anyone who refuse to go will pay fine.

Well, to go Pitakwa is not difficult thing. Instead of to pay fine, it is better to go to Pitakwa. After all person can still go to African Upwine Bar and chop *ngwo-ngwo* there, drink small *tombo* and make small jollity. So after two days, I went very early in the morning with small money in my pocket. I told my mother that I will return that very day. So my mother said good, but I must try and return oh, because she does not like all what she is hearing is happening outside. I asked her what she is hearing is happening outside but she said make I no worry. Just go to Pitakwa and return today that is all.

When I reached that Pitakwa everything which I saw

wondered me. Is this not the Pitakwa we are coming to every time? How can it change quick quick like this? Ehn? Everybody is very busy, running up and down, buying, selling, laughing, dancing, walking quick quick, pushing truck, driving motor, repairing bicycle, repairing motor, making shoe, chopping in hotel and bar. Everywhere people, motor-cycle, bicycle, lorry, car. *Shoo*! Even 'e remain small for me to confuse totally. If not to say I am very old man in Pitakwa sef I should have confused completely.

Now this meeting that I came to make is in the stadium. When I reach there, I find that porson don full am proper. All of them young young boys. They were talking how they want to go to army. How they have paid money to Okpara who will make sure that they join the army. As for me, I was very surprisised because I do not know that they used to pay money before they enter army. Even Zaza did not say that they paid money before to enter army. Why are they paying money now? Is this army special? Ehn? Why money? So I asked one of the boys who was talking about paying money why he have paid the money. Then the boy laughed and said that I do not know anything if I am asking that kain question. All the other boys begin to laugh. This thing pained me plenty. I was very angry with myself. Why am I living in that bush called Dukana where porson cannot even meet Okpara? Why am I living in that bush called Dukana where porson cannot even hear that they are paying money to Okpara before they join army? Then I remembered that Agnes is living in Dukana. It means that Dukana is good place. Plus why must porson pay money to enter into army? Is that a good army? But sometimes that is what they used to do, you know. So praps I am foolish after all? I begin to confuse again.

We were standing in that sun inside that stadium for long long time. Then I bought some groundnut and banana and chopped it while we were still waiting. Then they began to reach where we were standing. First they will measure somebody for chest. Then how tall he is. And so on. When it reached my turn they did not even measure me sef. They say I am too short to be soza. Too short to be soza? Am I not taller than Zaza? Even sef, am I not taller than all these boys they are taking to make soza? Is it because I have not paid money to Okpara? I was very very angry. As it was evening by this time, I begin to think I will return to Dukana. I moved out of the stadium. Immediately I saw some people looking right and clapping. Then I hear the same song which I heard before in the dream:

> My father don't you worry
> My mother don't you worry
> If I happen to die in the battlefield
> Never mind we shall meet again.

And the song was coming nearer and nearer. The people were clapping. Some of them were running to where the song was coming from. Still the song continue to come nearer and nearer. Then I saw the people who were singing it. Young young boys like myself, all of them with gun and uniform. It is that uniform that I like very much. When I see how they are all marching, prouding and singing, I am very happy. But when I see all their uniform shining and very very nice to see, I cannot tell you how I am feeling. Immediately, I know that this soza is wonderful thing. With gun and uniform and singing. And marching, left, right, left, right, my father don't you worry, left right, my mother don't you worry, left right. If I happen to die, right, in the battle left, never mind we shall meet again. Left right left right. They were marching, singing. And I was following them. And other boys too. Following them like *mumu*. Clapping. Enjoying ourself. I was thinking how I will be prouding when I join army like these boys. I continued to follow them till they reach where they are going. Then they do not allow us to enter where they are staying. They say we cannot enter there because we are not soza. I begin to vex. But I cannot leave that place because I want to see what the boys will do. I was still standing there when they finished everything plus saluting, then they all ran away to take their bath. Then they gave them food in better plate. I can see how the boys were eating, prouding, eating from better plate with meat and everything. I was jealousing them.

Late that evening, I began to return to Dukana. On the way, plenty of road block. Every time, they will ask us to come down from the lorry. Then they will search porson properly. And then they will search the motor too proper proper. Wasting porson time. For one place na soso young young girls were making the search. Even they asked me to remove my shoes sef so they will see if I am carrying gun or bomb. Touching my yarse and every place. I was very angry, you know, because it is not good for my persy to have woman giving me orders. Remove your hat. Remove your shoe. Come this way. All that type of nonsense. In this world? Can woman begin to command me like that? Am I a man or what? If they hear for Dukana that woman is commanding me will they not laugh at me?

As we entered the lorry again after the search by those girls, the people were saying that those girls are very clever. Very brave. They are making Simple Defence. Praps they too will go and fight and kill the enemy. Every time a porson will speak in that lorry he is always talking of the Enemy. The Enemy. The Enemy. I don't know what this person look like. Or *abi* is he like Hitla? But Hitla is white man. And the people are saying that the enemy is not very far away again. So he cannot be like Hitla.

Anyway, I have heard of new thing from this Pitakwa visit. There is one porson called Enemy that plenty people will go to kill. Plenty people including the girls. This Enemy na strong man. Even the big man speak about him that day when 'e come to the church for dream.

As we got nearer Dukana, I begin to vex when I think how those girls were giving me orders. I vex bad bad. I think I cannot have that nonsense again. I must go to join army immediately. I will wear uniform like those boys. I will sing those fine fine songs. Begin to march up and down, chop better chop. And as I am marching with gun and singing, prouding, all the people will come and look at me. They will say how I am brave man. Very brave man. Then Agnes will like me. And Zaza cannot make *yanga* for me again. And the thick man will know that inside my salt there is plenty of salt. And no woman whether Simple Defence or no Simple Defence cannot begin to give me order on the road like say I no sabi anything. And I will wear uniform!

LOMBER SEVEN

When I reached home that night, I cannot sleep because of thinking how I will get the money to give that Mr. Okpara so that he can take me as soza. Then before daybreak I said I must tell my mother about it.

As you know, my mother loves me very much. Since I began this apprentice work, she is the one who is always telling me what to do and what not to do. Even she is the porson who is paying my master to teach me. So I know that if I tell her that I want to be soza and I must pay this money to be soza she will do everything, even to sell her cloth and her farm, so I can be that soza. This mother is both father and mother to me. Every time I will be thinking of how when I am big man I must give her everything she wants because she is helping me too much.

So, that morning before she woke up from bed, I called her and told her I want to be soza and to be soza I must pay money to one Mr. Okpara. Look my trouble, oh. My mother did not even allow me to finish what I was saying. She said, 'Chiei! My son, God protect you from bad thing!' And small time, she begin to cry. Wonderful! What is wrong with my mother? How can she cry for something like this? Or have I said some bad word? I begin to beg her not to cry. I begged her for long time. Then before she can stop she told me to promise that I will not ask her that type of thing again. She wanted to give me juju. But I told her that juju is not necessary. So she went inside and draw water from the pot and give me to drink that early morning. I drank it all. Then she told me certain words. This is what she said:

'Look, Mene, you are my only son. Even I suffered plenty before I born you. I have born six of you, and you are the only one still alive. I want you to live and bury me when I die. I don't want to die like chicken, no burial. I have no father, no mother, no brother, no sister. You are my father, my mother, my brother and my sister. Do you hear me? Don't go and think of foolish thing. Go and think how you will marry and get picken who will be my proper son. You hear? If you want to marry now, I will pay the money. Today. I don't mind to sell my cloth and my farm to give you a wife. But this soza business is foolish nonsense.' That is what my mother said. Then she went away. Imagine!

I want to be soza my mother say I must marry. And no soza. So every day if I want to go to Pitakwa those girls on the road will always stop me, search my shirt, making their Simple Defence for me. Is it? So does my mother want me to be woman-man? So I am not like all those young young boys who are playing up and down, marching, singing, chopping better chop and wearing fine fine uniform with badge? Is it? So I will stay in this Dukana like Bom and Zaza? Even Zaza is better sef because he have gone to Burma. And he will always be giving me assault because I cannot go to soza as all my friends are doing. And I will just stay in Dukana without reaching Pitakwa, just borning children like rabbit. Is it? But can I disobey this my mother? Especially as na me be the only picken and already she is saying that I am her husband and brother and mother and father and sister and son? Me alone. So if I disobey her and run away, she will vex with me. And as she used to take care of me, true true, it is not good make I do something which will make her to vex with me, you know. And even sef, this marriage that she is asking me to marry, is it bad thing? If na Agnes that I will marry, it is not bad thing. But as Agnes have gone to Lagos, her people will be asking plenty money from anybody who want to marry her. Then where can we get the money to give to Agnes him people so that they will 'gree to make her to marry me? And how will I go and begin to say I want to borrow money to marry wife? I think the whole of Dukana will be laughing at me, if they hear that I am going to borrow money to marry wife. But sometime my mother fit find the money as she used to do her own thing. Because you know she is a very clever woman. With plenty farm and plenty trade and money otherwise she cannot pay the money so that I am apprentice driver.

So I begin to think, yes, I can try to make my mother happy. I will marry Agnes. That will make me to be happy too. So my mother and myself will be happy. Then we will try and make Agnes happy. She likes me to be soza. So she will tell my mother that unless I am soza, she will not marry me. Then my mother because she wants this picken, she must allow me to go to soza after I have married Agnes. Oh yes, that is a very good plan, you know. Very good plan. I was very happy by now, because I have made this good plan. And I know that when I tell people in Dukana that I will marry and then I will go to make soza, they will be talking about it and praising me as porson who get plenty sense.

But I must first tell Agnes that I want to marry her. As you know, if it is before before, it is not necessary for me to go and tell Agnes that I want to marry her. I for first tell my mother and then my mother will tell her mother and uncle as her papa is dead. And if they 'gree then we two will marry, after I have bought drink and paid the money. But not the girls of nowadays. And particularly this Agnes who have travelled to Lagos and is wonderful girl, beautiful like full moon in Dukana. I must tell her first and know if she will 'gree. Because although I think she like me, you know as they used to do in Lagos, she can fit to say she will not marry me. All these Lagos girls can make foolish *yanga*. Even, last time when I tell her that I will marry her, she asked me to go and be soza first. So praps she will not 'gree.

So, that night, I went to Agnes their house. She was very glad to see me, I think. "So you don't want to come to see me all this time, ehn?" she asked me.

"I travelled to Pitakwa," is what I answered.

"To Pitakwa? Why did you not come to take me with you? Or you think I don't like to go to Pitakwa? Ah, my dear, I am sure you went to see all those your concubines in African Upwine Bar."

I was laughing small small, smiling. This Agnes sef. How can she be talking like this? "I have no concubine in African Upwine Bar." I replied.

"Lie, lie man. You mean to say all this time you are going to Pitakwa you cannot find better woman wey you go dey take make small cooleh?"

"At all, at all. You know I am very good man."

"Good man? And every time your thing dey stand like snake wey no get house. Look as 'e dey stand even now sef."

Chei, this Agnes go kill porson oh. Why this girl dey speak like this? Ehn? Why? She no dey shame? This is what I was thinking to myself as Agnes was laughing plenty.

Her mama was not in the house. And her uncle too. That is why she was speaking like that. It is good too, because since she is speaking like that I can tell her all the things I want. If her Mama dey for house some time I no for fit tell am everything. And she too she will be shaming and cannot tell me anything freely. As you know, that is how girls used to behave in this Dukana.

"Agnes, I want to talk to you very serious," is what I said after some time.

Agnes begin to laugh again. I am telling you, when I see this girl as she is laughing, I begin to like her more. Because she is very very fine girl. Look as her teeth white like paper and her mouth small with black gum. Oh, I like this girl. Oh God, if you no 'gree make I marry this girl make I die one time. I was shaking inside my cloth. Then Agnes came and held my hand and begin to take me inside the house. As soon as we reach the house, she passed her hand round my neck and before I can count one two she put her lips into my mouth and her tongue begin to move inside my mouth. Jesus! I never see such sweet thing before oh. Is that how it used to sweet them inside cinema as they used to do every time? I did not know that it used to sweet like that when I was seeing it inside cinema as they were doing it many times. Oh God, is it? As the thing sweet me it is like say they put pin for my foot and the thing begin to run from my toe to my heart to my brain to the hair for my head. Oh, wonderful. So, after some time, Agnes removed her lips from inside my mouth. And then I told her that I love her, that I want to marry her whether she will 'gree to marry me. So that I will tell my mother and then she will come and tell Mama Agnes and then we can finish everything.

If na some other girl, Agnes would have been prouding. Sometime she will say 'I don't know' although she want to say 'yes'. But Agnes just tell me 'yes'. But she say I must be soza first. She say she wants to marry me quick quick so she can get her own house and born picken. Because she don tire for stay for another porson house. And she must get her own house quick quick. Even as I am the only picken of my mother, everything is awright. She will like to be my wife but she will marry me only if I am soza because she cannot marry any man who cannot defend her when trouble come.

So I told Agnes how I have determined to be soza because one, Zaza is prouding and giving me assault because I am not soza and two, because the thick man says Dukana boys must join soza to show that their own salt has salt inside it and three, because some girls who are making Simple Defence are giving me moless on the way to Pitakwa and four, because Agnes my lover say I must join soza and five, because of what the tall man was saying in the African Upwine Bar plus the fine fine uniform with badge which those young sozas were wearing in the army camp plus how Chief Birabee is smiling foolish idiot smile whenever 'e see soza. So Agnes said that she will be prouding of me very much when I am soza. Then I told her how my mother does not want me to be soza but to stay in the house and marry wife so that I can born picken as I am her one picken and she does not like that.

Then Agnes said, "Does it mean that if you are soza you cannot born picken again? You go fit born picken pass if you are soza. So your Mama does not know ehn? You wey your thing dey stand like snake wey no get house every time, how you no go fit born picken? Even you go born picken quick quick too as I see you."

This Agnes sef. She too like this talk of snake wey no get house. What kain girl be dis? So she told me make I no worry because when we don marry finish, she will tell my Mama wetin him want make him husband do. And she must 'gree.

As this Agnes was talking surprised me small, you know. She is very strong woman. Some time she will make stronghead too for house. I was still turning this thing for my mind when Agnes put her lips into my mouth and her tongue begin to move inside my mouth. Oh blessed Virgin Mary, no do dis kain thing to me, I beg you. I beg you. This thing too sweet, oh. Oh Agnes, I take God beg you, softly softly catch monkey oh. Softly, softly, I beg you.

So that night Agnes and myself sat together outside the house and we spoke about plenty things. To talk true, I cannot remember all the things we were speaking about because as you know, if two people are loving themselves they will be talking small small things. But it is not what they are talking that is important. It is what they are doing. That night Agnes and myself were enjoying. Enjoying plenty. And we were still enjoying when Agnes mama come to the house. When she saw me in the house she greeted me well well. That was a good thing because as you know, if she does not like me she will begin to hala because I am visiting her daughter very late in the night which is not good in Dukana. So when I saw how she is greeting me, I begin to think that when my mother will tell her that I love Agnes and I want to marry her she will 'gree and tell me to bring *tombo* and *ginkana* plus money so that I can marry her.

Because of this I was very happy when I was going home that night. I begin to thank God for how I went to the African Upwine Bar that night when I saw Agnes, the first time. I was thinking how I will be happy man when I have married Agnes. And how my mother will allow me to go to soza because I have married a girl who can give her picken. I know that my mother will be very happy.

*   *   *

Oh yes. My mama was very happy when I told her that I want to marry Agnes. And she was happy more than when she hear that Agnes have agreed to marry me. Because she wants plenty picken quick quick. When she spoke to Agnes mama there was no trouble at all. She paid the money or dowry for Agnes. We buy the drink and Agnes become my wife. She come begin to live with me and my mama. And I was very very happy because Agnes, the young beautiful Lagos baby with J.J.C. is now my own very wife. Oh, I was very happy and very proud.

LOMBER EIGHT

So one morning, Terr Kole, Bom, Duzia and Zaza were sitting in the playground talking as they used to do. I was passing to go and see Gbole my friend; I was thinking how I will greet all of them when immediately Duzia begin to hala for me. You know as Duzia used to talk. He cannot shame. Always shouting and laughing and talking anything that comes to his mouth. So as I was passing he shouted: "Sozaboy!"

I did not know that he was calling me. I just continued to walk as I was walking. And then I told them "Good morning, my masters." Instead they will answer as they used to do, all of them begin to laugh "*kwa kwa kwa kwa*." This thing was surprisising me because they cannot be laughing like that as soon as they see me unless they are talking about me before. And as you know, if they are talking about you like that in the playground, it means that they are thinking how they will kill you or make poison or juju so that either you will sick or you will die. Anyway, since Terr Kole is there, I cannot worry too much. Because everyone in Dukana knows that Terr Kole have never make juju or poison for anybody at all. So sometimes they are not speaking bad about me.

"Sozaboy!" Duzia was shouting again. "Don't you hear me, you? Sozaboy, còme here."

I begin to look everywhere because I think they are calling another porson.

"Don't look another place," Bom said, "don't look another place because you are the porson we are talking to. Do you think we are stupid, we don't know what is happening in this our town?"

"He thinks we are picken like himself," Zaza said, "You think that an old soza like myself will stay in this town and not know what is happening? Don't mind that all these foolish sozas of nowadays are beating me like dog and throwing me inside prison. I cannot answer them because I know that when the come comes to become, they cannot face old soza like myself who have conquered Hitla for Burma. So let me tell you, everything that is happening in this Dukana we know it well."

Then Duzia begin to laugh small small with the corner of his mouth.

"Well, Sozaboy, I'm sure you are fucking that girl well. Please don't tear her thing, oh. Because I know all you young young boys who have not seen *toto* before. When you see *toto* for the first time you will want to die before you leave it." That's what Duzia said.

"Are you enjoying it? I hear the girl can jam the thing well. Is it Lagos style she is using?" Bom asked.

Then Duzia replied quick quick, "I hear Sozaboy was shouting, begging her not to play like that or she will burst his *blokkus*."

Oh, this Duzia sef. Have you people ever seen man who useless like this? How can he be saying such thing? As I was saying, I cannot answer all this nonsense that these people are talking because to talk true I was shaming bad bad.

"Tell us, does the thing sweet you plenty? I know you will forget about all that your motor apprentice now begin to think of woman only and how to fuck every night," Zaza said.

"No. The boy knows what he is doing. You think he is a fool? You no see how he first go and marry the most beautiful girl in Dukana? Girl with J.J.C. who knows how to play well well inside the bed. The boy get plenty sense. Even sef he is going to be soza. Sozaboy, not so?" Duzia said.

"Oh yes, I know he will like to be soza. When he is soza that is when he will fuck pass with his long long *prick*. Ah, but Sozaboy, be careful oh. If you too do, you will not get woman to marry you again, like Zaza here. Don't you see, no woman in this Dukana can agree to marry Zaza again. All of them are saying that the man too do. He will tear woman toto quick quick. Anyway, you don marry now. But you must to be careful about this soza you want to be. Because it is not small thing," Bom replied.

"Ah, Sozaboy, you must to be careful oh. Because when you hear soza soza and you see Zaza going about in Dukana with loin cloth plus foto of white woman and woman's hair for him loin cloth, you will be thinking this soza is good thing. But I am telling you that it is not as easy as you are thinking because, . . ."

Duzia did not allow Zaza to finish speaking, before he said: "Yes, Sozaboy, you must to be careful. Because when you are making this soza in Burma or in the white man country, another porson can go and take this your fine fine young wife from you. Oh, it is not good for man to marry and then leave that woman to go and make soza. Oh no. And if that your woman just likes to open her leg for man, then she will just forget you when you turn your back. So you must to be careful about this soza you are going. Because there are plenty men in this Dukana carrying their *prick* like bamboo waiting for woman that they will chook, so you must to be careful about this soza you are going. Because many men will like to chook this fine fine girl you have married with plenty money."

Terr Kole did not say even one word at all. Even sef he does not laugh when they are talking all that nonsense that they are talking and laughing. He just sit down cool, no trouble. Even sef he does not smile. That is why everybody used to like Terr Kole. Young man or old man must like Terr Kole. Because he is gentleman proper. So when I see that he wants to speak I have to pay attention to him very carefully. Then this is what he said as I hear am.

"My son, I see that you have done a very big thing. To marry wife is not easy thing. Because anybody who marries wife have married trouble. And trouble no dey ring bell. And anybody who do something like that have done a very big thing. That is what I want to tell you. When I hear them saying everywhere that you have married that Lagos girl, I said to myself 'He is lucky boy, but he must to be careful.' Then I hear again how you are borrowing money to go and join army. I think it is a good thing. Because I do not like to hear that in the whole of the army there is not even one Dukana boy. Does it mean that our own children cannot make soza? If Zaza here joined army twenty years ago and fight strong man like Hitla, conquer him and bring salt to Dukana why cannot young man go and fight now? So it is good thing that you are going to make soza. But you must to be careful. Because when you see Zaza here holding foto of fine woman, and walking about with loin cloth and fine fine scent, you must not think it is easy like that. So you must to be careful. Because soza man life na *waya*. Is it not so, Zaza?"

Zaza begin laugh one kind laugh as if to say, 'make 'e go try now, make we see.'

"So you must to be careful. Because soza is not just to marry new wife dey enjoy. It is not every soza who goes to fight who return as 'e go. Is it not so, Zaza?"

Zaza begin laugh small laugh again for de corner of him mouth. 'E no talk at all, dis time. 'E just dey laugh one small cunny laugh wey I no fit understand.

"So you must to be careful. Because war is not small thing. Anyway, I know you will do well because you are careful young man." That is what Terr Kole said in the end.

When he finished then Duzia started again. He was laughing as he was talking. "Terr Kole, you have plenty of time to spend on this boy, oh. Do you think he is listening to you? Don't you see how his eye is full of sleep? He did not sleep last night, you know. Just beating that woman *toto* like drum, that's all. Oh, you bloody fucking bastard dog, if you don't leave that little girl alone, thunder will tear you to hundred pieces."

Then Bom said, "Awright, you, Sozaboy fucker, you better go now and prepare yourself. But as you are fucking this your new wife, do not forget those of us who are suffering here with old old *kpongoss* woman with dry yarse."

Look ehn, this Duzia and Bom are nonsense people, you know. That is what I was thinking as I leave them. Do you hear how they are talking? It is good thing that this Duzia cannot walk, you know. Because if he can walk as he is talking, he will make plenty trouble for Dukana. Even sef, the man no get any work to do, just to go about knacking tory and making people to laugh. When I think of what Bom and Duzia are saying, I laugh plenty plenty, although I cannot laugh before because of Terr Kole and because they will think I am prouding, no respect for old people because I have married young, beautiful Lagos girl.

So from that time wherever I go people are calling me 'Sozaboy,' 'Sozaboy'. Even I am very famous in Dukana sef. All the young young men are saying that I am tough man. Marrying fine Lagos girl, just like that and then preparing to go and join army. They are saying that after some time they will give me proper big position for the army. Myself, I was prouding plenty. When they call me 'Sozaboy' I will answer well well. Even I begin to tell people that my name is Sozaboy. If I go to any porson house and I knock and that porson asks who is that, I will answer 'Sozaboy'. I like the name well well.

Agnes for the house was another woman altogether. She does not talk all that snake house as she used to talk before we marry. She just like to do her house-work, helping my mother in the farm and in preparing food. My mother was prouding plenty because her picken have now married fine fine girl. And when she goes out she must commot with Agnes so that people will see that she is her in-law. Every time she will be telling Agnes that she must get belly quick quick because after all she is fine fine girl and all fine girl with young husband must get picken, fine boy picken.

I will not tell you a lie. I myself I was very happy too. Not only prouding because I marry fine wife. But as you know any porson wey marry wife new new must be happy. In the morning oh, in the night. Every time when I see Agnes in the afternoon as she is walking, I will be glad. I see her J.J.C. and her small buttocks moving up and down. And I will be thinking to myself 'so all this J.J.C. and fine fine bottom na my own ehn?'

As I was saying before, all this time I am not working again, because my master motor still dey for garage. Even I no worry about the motor since Agnes dey for house. Every time when my friends see me on the road in Dukana, they are saying 'Ah, this Sozaboy na woman rapa proper. Always with him new wife'. When Agnes hear as they are talking, she does not like it at all. One day, she told me, "I think you have to go to soza soon. All this fighting, strong man like you cannot stay in the house. And everybody in Dukana is saying that you cannot fight again because you don marry. I do not like that kain talk."

"Very good," is what I answered. "You know that I myself want to go to army. But you know as my mother is thinking about this soza business."

"Never mind. I will tell her what I want my husband to do. That's all."

Many days passed and I did not hear anything again only they are saying that the war have started and that our sozas are doing very well. Killing the enemy like fly. But all that one is talk. In Dukana, nobody is worrying about the war. Only there is no salt. The people do not like that at all. Then Pastor Barika is preaching everyday that the world will soon end. In the morning he will say that the world will end in the night. And in the night he will say that the world will end in the morning. Everyday. Then after some time all the churches in Dukana begin to make open-air prayer meeting begging God to take smell of war from Dukana. All the Pastors plus Apostles are saying that if they pray well, the war will not come to Dukana because after all Dukana is at the end of the world.

So after the prayer, everything is going on as before. Chief Birabee is going everywhere taking money and chop from the women so that they will hear the name of Dukana in the radio as he used to say. And Zaza is going everywhere with him loin cloth and big big belly. And Bom, everyone is now calling him BBC because na him sabi the news of the war pass, is everyday saying how our sozas are killing the ENEMY like fly. Even Bom will give the number who have died sef. But that is all. Dukana cannot care what is happening. They are not planning what they will do if the fighting reaches Dukana. I say to myself again Dukana will see pepper if the war enter it. But as the war is far far I think some times it will not reach Dukana as everybody is saying. But I know that whether the war reach Dukana or not, I must be soza so that I can wear uniform.

So one day I called my mother and told her that I must join soza immediately. Immediately my mother heard that one she begin to cry. She cried till her eyes red like pepper. But she cannot talk to me that I will not go because when she complained to my wife about how every time I am telling her that I want to go to soza and she does not like it, my wife begin to cry till her eye red like pepper. So I was standing in the middle of two women who were crying with their eyes red like pepper, because of my joining soza. But my mother after all just surrender one early morning. Agnes and myself we were sleeping when my mother knocked in our room. So we dressed up quick quick and opened the door. Then my mother entered the room and sat down on the bed between Agnes and myself. This is what she said:

"Now, my son, and you, my daughter. You two are man and wife today. I thank God. I know how it is between a man and his wife. You eat together, you sleep together, you plan together. I pray that God will bless you two because you are young. And give you plenty picken. When husband and wife 'gree on one thing, that is all. Since you entered this house, my daughter, I have seen how you behave yourself. You are good girl. I thank God. You do not have stronghead like other girls. And anything I tell you, you like to do. Your husband says he will go to soza. I do not like it, but you and your husband like it. I do not like it because I cannot understand this soza palaver. If it is to fight in Burma or far far place, I can understand it, even if I do not like it. But if war is coming, it is better to be in your own house and fight it. Better to die sef in your own house if you are going to die. And all this die die die, I don't like it. God make us to live. All this fighting bring trouble and make people to die. I do not like it. Young young people dying. And if that porson who dies is your only son, it is not a good thing, oh God. Well my son, you say you want to go to make soza. What I can say is God protect you. Not everybody who goes to war will return. But not everybody will die. I want you to return to me. Do you hear? I want you to return." Then she went to her room and brought out a bundle of money.

"You say you need money to pay before you can become soza. Here is the money."

Then she went and brought water in a cup and took me to the door of the house. She poured the water on my leg. She said: "You were born here. You must return here. And return walking by your leg: Yes, my son, return with both leg. Because I am your mother. I am the one who born you. I want you to return to me." She poured the water on my leg again. Then she went away.

I did not see my mother the rest of that day as I was preparing to go. That preparing to go no be any big thing at all. Because I no get box and not to say I will carry food. Just to say goodbye to everybody. That's all.

In the town I was telling everybody, prouding, that I am now going to soza tomorrow. That I will fight the Enemy to nonsense. That I will bring plenty things back to Dukana afterwards. And whenever I talk, the people are looking at me like I am wonderful porson and saying 'Sozaboy'. Oh I was prouding, very happy. I begin to like this Dukana more than. All those houses begin to fine for my eye. The plantain and banana and orange trees which I can see everywhere begin to shine for my eye. Even the road as it is full of sand sand begin to look like road that is going to heaven. And when I think of the people like Duzia and Bom and Terr Kole and all the others and how they were always speaking, and how I will not be in Dukana to hear them making joke all the time, I was very very sad at all.

"Sozaboy, Sozaboy, so you want to leave us and no drink ehn? Is it? Do you think you are the first Dukana man to go to soza? See Zaza here. Have he not gone to soza before? Before he went to that him Burma, don't you know he bought drink for us and for Sarogua? If not so, do you think he will return to Dukana after killing Hitla and fucking Hitla's daughter from morning till night for three months? You young people of nowadays don't know anything at all. This drink that you are seeing, whether palm wine or *ginkana*, is a very big thing you know. Don't forget it anywhere you are. Take small whether in bottle or calabash. Always. It is a good friend. Very good friend. Whether you are happy oh or not happy. Whether you are tired or strong. If you get woman or when you don't get woman. It is a good friend, I am telling you. Always keep him by your side." That is what Bom said. He and Duzia and Zaza were in our house.

"Where is your mother?" Duzia asked. "I know she will be hiding so she cannot give us drink today that her son is going to soza. Awright let her hide. Shit. Well, we have brought you drink, you Sozaboy fucking bastard dog. Where is that your fine fine girl? Let her bring us some cup for drinking."

So Agnes who was inside the kitchen brought cups. As soon as Duzia saw her, his eyes were looking like *mumu*. Until Agnes left the room.

"He! Sozaboy, you get big eye oh. Zaza, you see the kind of woman this little boy is marrying? You see her breasts like calabash. And that bottom. Oh, if better man puts his prick into tnat bottom, he will see Jesus Christ. Ha! Sozaboy, what fine dish you are going to leave behind for other people! Anyway, this night you must chop as you have not chopped before. Ha! ha!"

"Awright, awright, Duzia. That will do," said Zaza. "Awright, I say. As old soza, I say awright. Today is special day. As this our son, this Sozaboy fucker is leaving us to join soza. It is wonderful thing. I remember those days in Burma. Oh. But today is not for that. We have already spoken to Sozaboy. We have told him he must to be careful. Now it is for us to tell Sarogua to protect this our boy. Ach, Sarogua! You must guide this your picken. You know how you brought me out of that forest of Burma safely, even giving me better wife to marry. Now you must be with this Sozaboy. Bring him back to Dukana on his two legs. Not on his back. Don't be angry with him because he is only a young boy. Bring him back, Sarogua, bring him back safely."

Then Zaza poured drink on the ground.

"You speak well. Very well." Bom said. "Now pour the drink down the throat of those of us who are still living."

So they began to drink. All the time they were drinking, they did not speak at all. The glass was passing from Bom to Duzia then to Zaza then back to Bom then to myself. They did not speak at all which was very surprisising as every time you see Dukana people drinking, they must be shouting and singing until they finish the drink. Then they began to sing.

> They have beaten him, oh, oh, oh
> They have beaten him, oh
> Porson wey no get power
> Make 'e no go war

Then they began to sing again

Kaiza run away
Kaiza run away
Kaiza run away
Because of fear of sozas
Kaiza run away
Kaiza run away
Because of fear of sozas.

Bom and Zaza began to dance. As Duzia cannot dance, he was just sitting down, shaking his body, up and down, shaking up and down. As they were singing, many other men who were passing, heard them and they came to our house. Some people bring drink; so everybody was singing, drinking and dancing in that Dukana until very late that night. Even sef it was midnight before they left our house.

Early next morning when the motor was ready to go to Pitakwa I just woke up. All that night Agnes and myself were lying together. She was holding me very tight. When I told her that it is time for me to go away, she hold me tight more than. Then she began to cry. I can feel the water from her eye as it was running on my shoulder. Then after some time I just say, "Okay my dear, I will return. Okay." So I left her and went and knocked on my mother's door. The door was not locked. I pushed it open. My mother was lying on the bed facing the wall. At first I thought she was sleeping. Then I called her softly. "Dada." She turned round. She was crying plenty. Then I told her that I am going away to Pitakwa to join soza. She did not answer one word only to call me with her hand. When I came near the bed she held me very near to herself. She was crying plenty plenty.

As I walked to the motor my mother and my wife Agnes were standing in front of the house, holding each other. They were crying plenty.

Day never break proper yet. But the women of Dukana have begin to take their pots to carry water. Otherwise everything was quiet as before. As the motor was leaving Dukana, I was thinking to myself how everything is quiet in Dukana. All the houses were staying as before. I think it is good as everything is quiet and going on as usual. It is good for Agnes and for my mother.

LOMBER NINE

By this time I have paid Okpara the money that he wanted and I am already soza although no uniform yet. When they asked my name I just tell them 'Sozaboy'. I think they like the name because everyone is calling me 'Sozaboy' all the time whether they get something to tell me or not. And I was prouding plenty too.

Not just because they are all calling me 'Sozaboy,' Sozaboy'. But because I am now soza true true. By this time, they have cut our hair so that my head was shining like moon. Then they give us, all of us, P.T. although they do not write P.T. for the back pocket as they used to do. Then they give us canvas shoe. So that every time when we are running, you will see us with shining head wearing only P.T. and no singlet or shirt with canvas shoe running and sweating.

Every day very early morning we must be running and we are singing as we are running. This running is not just small small oh. We can run long long way every time. And as you are running na so dem dey beat you. Just dey hala for we head. 'E get one man, San Mazor, na so everyone dey call am. That man sabi wicked. Always if porson come late even by one minute he must beat him well well. But even all that beating and trouble no make me to not to enjoy what we are doing. Na that standing for line wey I like pass. All of us in one straight line. Then the San Mazor will just shout 'Quashun!' and all of us will move our right leg and stamp it on the ground 'gbram'. No other movement at all. If any porson just move, the San Mazor will just shout well '*Tan Papa dere.*' This '*Qua Shun*'! and '*Tan Papa dere*' were very confusing at first. We cannot understand what they mean. But anyway we know that when the San Mazor call 'quashun' we must move right foot and make '*gbram*' and we no move at all if 'e shout '*Tan Papa*'. And when he shout '*Ajuwaya*' then we can stand and scratch or do anything. After some time we were all calling the San Mazor '*Tan Papa*'. Every day we will be making all this '*quashun*' and '*tan papa*' and '*ajuwaya*' for almost one week, plus running and singing early in the morning. Then we chop. Three times everyday. After that, we begin to march. Left right, left right, left right. About turn! Right turn! Plus '*hoping udad mas*'. This '*hoping udad mas*' used to please me plenty oh. As soon as we hear that '*hoping udad mas*' then those in the front line plus those in the back line will move front and back one two three, *gbram*! Oyibo! Oh, I cannot tell you how this thing was making me happy. Tan Papa say that after we know how to march properly, then they will give us uniform.

It is this uniform that I am waiting for. As soon as I have it, I will know that I am soza proper. So we continued to march up and down making '*quashun*' and '*ajuwaya*' and '*tan papa dere*' and '*hoping udad mas!*' Then after about one month, one fine day, they called us to the store. And gave us uniform. Oh how I am prouding because of this uniform! Look how it is strong and can stand by itself. And when I wear it, it fits me *helele*. In fact I am thinking as I am wearing that uniform for the first time how Agnes will feel if she sees me inside it. I believe that she will be prouding of me. And if Zaza and Bom see it, they will also be prouding because Dukana boy is now inside new fine soza uniform.

Then after that uniform we were still marching up and down, up and down, left right, left right, left right, some times they will take us to the town and we will march prouding through the town and singing:

> My mother don't you worry
> My father don't you worry
> If I happen to die in the battlefield
> Never mind we shall meet again.

Myself, when we reach that place where they say 'my father don't you worry' I must say 'my Agnes don't you worry' for my mind, because as you know in the army you cannot say what you like. You must obey and do what they ask you to do. And I will be looking round to see whether any porson who knows me or porson from Dukana is seeing me as I am marching and throwing up my hand and singing well well. And when I see all those 'Simple Defence' people whether man or girl I will be prouding because now I am soza and they cannot search me as they were doing before before. And in the evening when we go to Upwine Bar as before, everyone will be respecting myself and the other sozas. Even they used to give us drink free of charge because as they talk, na we dey make the country to strong and good. So I was very very happy at all.

But only one thing remain. Because as I hear them talking it, khaki no be soza. Not because you are wearing khaki with picture on the hand that you will think you are soza. Because any porson can still beat you and you cannot do him anything. So before any porson can say he is soza, that porson must have gun. This gun is number one for soza. So I was thinking to myself that until I get gun I cannot be proper soza. Every time I will be asking my friend, one boy we used to call Bullet, when they will give us gun. Then he will answer that they will give us gun when we have learnt how to shoot it.

"And which time will they learn us how to shoot the gun?" I used to ask Bullet.

"One thing at a time and that well done." That is what Bullet will always say. I cannot understand what he means but this Bullet is proper book man. Every porson is saying that he should be soza captain not just soza. Sometime they will make him sarzent quick quick because he knows book proper proper. So anyway I continued to wait so that they will give us gun afterwards and then I will be soza proper.

So we were marching and singing for long time. Then we begin to use stick. This stick is like gun. When we are holding it, it is because there is no gun and we do not know how to use gun. So we must first make practice with the stick. To talk true word, I do not like this stick palaver. Am I stick soza or soza proper? Any porson can use stick afterwards. Stick cannot make man soza. If they want us to be soza proper, they must give us gun quick quick. That is what I was saying in my mind. Because as you know, when you are soza inside the army you cannot be complaining otherwise they give you punishment. If you see how I was suffering because of how I came late to parade one morning, you will sorry for me. Just a few minutes late, you know. Tan Papa make me do double quick march for more than thirty minutes. I am telling you, by the time I finished that double quick march, water was running from my body like River Jordan. I was shitting inside my trouser and I cannot talk to anybody at all. Oh God, what type of trouble is this, ehn? Is it so for this soza work? Even, not only that double quick march oh. Afterwards they take me to the guard room. They beat me. They shave my head *mala*. No better chop sef. I am telling you this thing is no joke at all. I was seeing pepper throughout. From that time I say to myself that I will always do the correct thing for this soza work. Because I cannot go to guard room again, begin to suffer and piss inside my trouser as before.

So I continued to carry stick with them. Every time they will shout 'udad arms' and 'solope arms.' I like this 'udad arms' and 'solope arms' because when they shout it, then all of us will move the stick up to our shoulder or from the shoulder to the ground. And we will be knocking our feet on the ground *gbram.*' It was very very interesting.

Then they begin to show us how we can shoot gun. But as na only Tan Papa hold the gun, all of us will only be watching him. Every time Tan Papa will tell us to respect the gun: 'Because, as you see the gun, it is not small thing. If soza will live or die, it is gun. Don't joke with am. Love am, respect am, keep am clean every time. Don't allow cold to catch it. Love it as you love your picken; as you love your wife, as you love your girl friend. Sleep with am as you sleep with your wife or your girl friend. No do anything wey fit make the gun to vex. Because as you see it, even though you aim it at another porson, and the gun no like you, and you no handle am well and the gun begin vex, it can refuse to kill the porson you have aimed at and instead kill you to spirit.' This is what Tan Papa is always saying.

You know as this Tan Papa used to teach us is very good. The man no sabi book but he know how to teach something and you will enjoy it. Some of the boys are saying that he is old soza before in Burma. Others say that he was a soza captain before but they removed the button from his shoulder because he fight and he cannot defend himself because of bad English that he will always be speaking. But myself I like the man. Because of the way he used to talk to me and treat us with better sense. I think that if I near the man well, he will be giving me better advice every time. And I think Tan Papa like me too. Because every time he will be calling me and sending me message. So I used to buy kola and drink for him after we have finished our work. Then he will ask me to sit down and he will ask me why I join soza and whether I like the training which they are giving us. So I will tell him how I am happy that I am soza because of the uniform and the fine fine chop we are eating everyday. And how I like to be marching up and down and singing every time. So he asked me whether that is all. And I told him I like to show my wife who loves me plenty that I am brave man who can defend her in time of trouble like this. Then Tan Papa asked me one kain question which I cannot understand. "This your wife wey want you to be soza suppose your hand or your leg cut, do you think she will still want to marry you?" Believe me yours sincerely, I have not asked this type of question before. Even sef, why my leg or hand go cut? Why 'e go cut? I ask Tan Papa why him think my leg go cut or my hand? So he said that he did not say that my hand will cut. Only he was asking whether my wife will still marry me if my hand cut. "Because war is war, you know," is what he said at last.

The whole of that night, I did not sleep well. I was thinking how Tan Papa said 'because war is war you know'. What is this war? Is it not soza and soza, gun and gun? That is what these old sozas are always doing. Like Zaza, they think because they have fought before no porson can fight again.

So I was saying to myself that what Tan Papa is saying cannot matter. That even if I return from the soza without leg, Agnes will still marry me. Ehn? But will she still marry me? If I no get leg and hand, why will I still want to marry woman? Look. This type of thinking can kill porson you know. So I begin to do everything so that I will not think like that again. But I cannot forget from that day how Tan Papa was saying because war is war.

All this time they were saying that the war is becoming more serious every day. But in that Pitakwa we were very far away from war. Because as we were not hearing the sound of gun we cannot know that they are fighting at all. So we continued to make our training with stick, no gun. Everyone was asking when they will give us gun. We were still asking when one day Tan Papa said that we will get gun tomorrow. We were all very happy to hear that. We jumped up, all of us and begin to dance up and down. So at last we will get gun. And be sozas proper.

Then Tan Papa said we must dress well well, and polish our shoe well well too because the Chief Commander General is coming to see us. For what for? Anyway, Tan Papa said it is very good. Because it is only when the sozas are good that the Chief Commander General by himself will come to see them. Even sef the Chief Commander General can make porson soza captain or sarzent or corple right in the field during parade. Because he is very important porson. Na him get all the uniforms, all the buttons and ropes and all the sozas. He is the number one of the sozas. Sometimes he is better than Hitla sef. At least he can fight better.

So all of us were very very happy to hear that the Chief Commander General was coming to see us and we have to prepare well well for am. With shining shoes and cloth that they have pressed well proper.

So we begin to march and stand for attention and make 'Hopen udad mas' and 'solope arms' and 'udad arms'. Ha, it was very very interesting. Then after some time they bring every man one gun. Look ehn, I was very surprisised when I see that gun and I hold it for my hand. I am telling you, I was holding the gun with plenty of respect and love as Tan Papa was telling us before. Even not anything else sef but as the gun was shining and when I think of the things that it can do. That day I was prouding plenty because it means that I am now soza proper. That night, they took the gun from us. But I was only thinking of the gun and how Tan Papa said we should sleep with it and love it like wife. Anyway, they have taken the gun away and I cannot sleep with it. But I know that one day, they will give us to take home and sleep with it.

Then the morning after, we begin very early to prepare because that day the Chief Commander General will be coming to see us. All our uniform was shining well well like the sun that day. All the boys were smiling proud proud and Tan Papa too when he saw how we were looking was laughing with everybody. He told Bullet "You try plenty, you try." Then he told me, "You do well, small boy soza, you do well, Sozaboy." And everybody in the line was laughing because of how he was calling us. So all of us were very happy.

After we have marched small and stood in line, then one big man came and gave us command, left right, and solope arms and udad arms and hopen udad mas and qua shun and ajuwaya. Very very tough man. He was shouting plenty. Tall man. Speaking fine fine English. "You boys must be smart. Salute properly. Behave like soldiers. Season soldiers." To tell the truth, I cannot understand everything he was saying. But as I see 'am, I am proud to be soza with gun. I think that one day I will be like that soza with spectacle, tall and fine speaking with brass band voice, enjoying myself inside fine car and fine house, giving command to small boys who are just entering new into soza life.

Then he begin to march all of us. Even Tan Papa was marching too. Power pass power. Now Tan Papa no be important man again. Then we stopped marching. The sun was still shining plenty. We were sweating like no man business. When will the Chief Commander General come? We were standing in the hot sun.

After some time, I think the sun begin to shine proper proper. My eyes were turning when one fine fine car come in with loud noise. I was looking well well to see whether the Chief Commander General was inside the car. But not only one car, oh.

Plenty of motor and car. Then they begin to come down. Fine fine tall men in fine fine uniform. Then that big man with brass band voice begin to give us order again, *Solope arms*, Present arms. *Udad arms. Qua shun.* Everything. By this time, Tan Papa is like ourselves – very small man at all. He cannot talk at all. Power pass power. So the big man with brass band voice begin to march to the Chief Commander General as I think. Then he saluted him. This Chief Commander General is not very big man you know. I did not see him well because we were marching and marching and marching. Making Passing Out Parade as they call it. I was very tired by the time that the Chief Commander General was looking at all of us as we stand in line. When he came near me, he did not stop at all. I don't know whether he was seeing all of us who were standing in that line. I do not think he was seeing us at all. Then after he have looked at all of us in the line, he went back and then we all made 'stand at hais' so that he can begin to speak to us.

In fact, ehn, the man was speaking like that D.O. was speaking in the dream for Dukana. Using big big words that I cannot understand. But every time he will be calling that Enemy. I begin to fear this Mr. Enemy you know. Because I am thinking he must be strong man pass Hitla sef. Otherwise why is everyone talking about him? Even the Chief Commander General is fearing this man. Why? Even sef, why all of us will join hand to kill him. Does he have many heads? What is wrong with him? 'E get stronghead? Or did he call another man's wife? Why does everybody want to kill him? And why they will train plenty people to kill him? All these things were wondering me as the Chief Commander General was speaking. "You boys have got excellent training. You must be brave and proud of your country." Fine fine grammar. "We shall overcome. The Enemy will be vanquished. God is on our side."

So this Chief Commander General is also Church man, ehn? Is it? So he is speaking about God like Pastor Barika too? So what is that Pastor Barika doing in Dukana now now? Is he telling the people that the world will soon end? Or is he making prayer, shouting early in the morning in the church and in the town square as usual? And Terr Kole, Bom and Zaza, what are they doing now? That Chief Birabee is he still smiling idiot smile for Dukana when he sees sozas? Oh, I think I must go to see that Dukana where my Agnes is living so that she can see me in my uniform with gun and then she will be prouding of me because I am now Sozaboy proper.

So I was still thinking of all this when I heard everybody shouting 'Hooray' with their hat in their hand for air. So I myself joined them in shouting that 'hooray'. You know as soza thing is. You must do as everybody is doing. So we all shouted 'hooray'. And when I looked at the boys some of them were crying with plenty of water coming from their eyes.

When we reached the dormitory I was asking Tan Papa why the boys are crying. So he said it is because the Chief Commander General said that the Enemy is tired for the fight and so therefore all the training we are getting cannot be used at all. We cannot get anybody to shoot and kill. So I was not very happy to hear that.

I think I have to join the boys to cry.

LOMBER TEN

God no gree bad thing! We were still sleeping when Tan Papa say we must all get up. Quick quick. I wake up wipe my eye. Everybody was getting up. Tan Papa was hallering like madman. 'Get up you fucking bastard idiot. Get up you bugger'. And he was kicking everybody with his shoes. 'You think sozaman get bed for sleep? Una don sleep for last time today. Get up bastard bugger, God don punish your *prick*.' This is what Tan Papa was saying. Many times. Until all of us wake up begin to tie our blanket and waterproof. Myself, I was very confuse. But you know as soza thing is. You cannot ask question. Only to obey. That's all. So Tan Papa say we must stand in line. We stand in line. He say everybody must take all him thing from that place because we are going on long journey. Ha! So we all entered the lorry. Then Tan Papa told us to go well. Before the motor commot, he told me: "Sozaboy, go well, you hear. Remember, war is war." Even I cannot talk to him. I was very confuse. So, as any time I am confused, I must ask Bullet what is happening. He said we are going for front. This Bullet is a clever boy, but he can be stupid some time you know. What he mean by we are going for front? No be inside lorry we dey? So I told Bullet that I know that we are going for front. But where are we going to as we are going this front? Then he begin to laugh. 'E say, 'Sozaboy, you don't know anything yet'. And 'e begin laugh again, small small.

So the motor continue to move front for front. As we are travelling in the night, no light anywhere, I cannot see where we are going sef. I begin to remember how Zaza was telling us when he was going to Burma about no light inside the lorry. He does not know where he is going at all. Praps na Burma we dey go, oh. No. Bullet no fit call Burma front. Na one place dem dey call FRONT we dey go. Wetin we dey go do dere? God alone sabi. Especially as Mr. Enemy don die finish and we no go shoot am again. And we do not hold gun sef. Ha! Anyway, we continue to travel inside the motor. Even some of the sozas begin to sleep again with their blanket and waterproof for their back inside the lorry. And we were travelling like this till day begin break small small.

By this time I do not know where we are again because even if you look outside you cannot see anything except bush and forest. I begin to think of that time they were carrying soza to Burma and I was saying to myself that sometimes they are carrying all of us to Burma where we are going to fight proper Hitla as our own Hitla who they call Enemy have decided not to fight again as that Chief Commander General was telling us yesterday. So I was even prouding to myself because after everything said and done I am going to fight for Burma and Zaza cannot be prouding for me again as he was doing before before.

And I was thinking how I will kill Hitla plenty time and then when I don kill am plenty, I will marry his daughter and not just to marry and leave her for Burma as Zaza do, oh. I must bring the woman to Dukana so that people will talk how I am clever boy. But what of Agnes? Oh, I will tell her that this my wife is win-the-war-wife so she must not vex because she know that man must marry two, three or four wife, as him hand reach. Some time by that time Agnes will not be J.J.C. again so I will tell her that it is good for young man, like old man, to get new wife, proper J.J.C., every time so that his blood can change. I think Agnes will understand and she will take this my wife, Hitla's sister, like her own sister. If they quarrel, I must settle the quarrel quick quick. So when I think of all this, I begin to glad small small. I begin to proud too as soza from Dukana and how we are going to fight for Burma. So as I was thinking all this thing, the lorry come stop.

No sooner, than one man jump from inside the bush begin to

order all of us to get down from the lorry. So we begin get down quick quick; we were carrying our waterproof plus our waterbottle. Then they ask us to enter one line. And then begin to march us, left right, left right, softly softly. The man no dey shout as dem dey do for parade. Just softly softly. Left right, left right. This thing wonder me, oh. We were marching like this until we come near one place where we see plenty canoe and water. Canoe and water. Some of the boys begin to make complain. They were saying that they have not seen water before. That if they fall inside that water they cannot swim. Even I saw one boy as his mouth was shaking *helele* like say 'e get fever. The boy begin cry, dey move back small small, like say him want run go back. So I was saying to myself that this boy is stupid boy. How 'e go run back? To where? For wetin? Why him dey fear? Common water? And all of us are going to enter canoe. So why him alone go fear? So I told him not to fear like that because it is not good for soza to cry. And Tan Papa go vex if he see soza wey him don train begin to cry because of water. If porson dey fear because of blood, 'e fit be good thing. But as for water, soza, better soza no fit cry because of water.

Then they tell us to enter the canoe. We enter the canoe one by one. By this time, day don break well well. It was raining too, small small. That rain was not good for the body. We all entered the canoe. They give us paddle and we begin to paddle the canoe. We entered the mangrove. The toads were singing everywhere. But I do not hear the sound of any bird. Only toad. I am telling you, this thing fear me small. Because toad singing is not sign of good omen. And you know how bad this toad singing can be. Like say porson die. And by this time, every place come dark again because of the tall mangrove and other trees. The daybreak never reach inside the mangrove.

So we begin to turn turn inside those canoes. From one bend corner to another bend corner. Through mangrove and more and more forest. The toads all shouting like say dem dey sing for church. All of us, nobody is talking. Even myself, I cannot sing all those few fine song they have taught us before and which I think I will like to sing always. As everybody was silent was not good. So I ask Bullet why everybody is quiet like that. He does not want to answer me. Ha!

At last, we come reach the place we dey go. I know say na the place because they have cut all the bush in that area, begin put tent. And even they are cooking inside big pot there. By this time, day don break proper and we fit see everybody well. We were still sitting inside the canoes. So the man who took us into the canoe first jumped down and begin to march to the tent. I was watching him very carefully. When he reached there he saluted smartly. Then he and the man inside the tent begin to speak. I cannot hear what they were saying. But after some time this soza captain saluted the man inside the tent again. Then he begin to march towards us. Then he told us to get down from the canoes. All of us came down. The water was inside our shoe and up to the knee. Some of the boys begin to try to remove them shoe and socks. So the soza captain shouted to them 'don't be silly!' That what do we think, because water get inside our shoe we begin to remove the shoe. Do we think we are in our mama kitchen? If we do not want water to touch our shoe how will we do when we begin to sleep inside the water?

So now, all the boys were very very surprisised when they heard this one. Sleep inside the water? Whasmatter? Even myself I was very very angry. Why this soza captain is trying to frighten everybody? He knows that nobody can sleep inside water. So how can he speak like this? *Abi*, the man think that all of us are foolish, ehn? Just because he is soza captain? Well, we go see. That is what I was saying to myself. And I was still speaking like this when some sozas begin to march to where we were standing. They were going inside the canoe from where we have just come from. They were laughing small small and looking at us. I no like as dem dey laugh. So they marched into the canoe and sat down and pull the canoe commot. Then I think one thing to myself. Those who are going away are laughing. Those who are coming in, some are crying. Is this a good thing at all? Then I remembered what Tan Papa used to say. War is war. As I was thinking all this I heard 'Qua Shun'. Everybody stiff him hand by himself.

Then the soza captain told us that we are there to stop enemy from formfooling. He said, as I hear am, that we must do as we are told. He said we must not make noise, we must do as our leader tell us. He said many other things. But as you know, soza cannot listen to everything soza captain is saying. Even if he listen, he cannot understand everything. So as I have heard one or two, I can take that one go sleep. Enemy must not formfool. And we must obey our leader.

But I no sleep that day. We no sleep at all. We *just* dey work, work, work. De soza captain first ask us to put our waterproof and sack on the ground. Then everybody take matchet and begin to cut the grass and trees. When we don clear the ground finish we begin dig pit. Every place na soso pit. As we were digging, I was asking Bullet for what we shall use the pit for. Bullet said that we shall sleep inside the pit. Sleep, inside pit? Oh my mother who born me! Have you seen what is happening to Sozaboy? Sleeping inside pit. I did not like that at all. Anyway, we finished digging the pits. Small pits everywhere facing different directions. They said three people will be inside one pit. As we were digging, I was thinking to myself that it is like burial ground. Because porson fit enter there, and when that porson die, they will just cover him with the sand from inside the pit. Because we did not throw the sand away. We just put it for the mouth of the pit, so that if you are inside that pit, anybody who is coming from the other side, or looking from the other side, will not see you. I am telling you, many things were crossing my mind as we were digging those pits. We were digging when the sun commot. We were digging when the sun was shining proper and you cannot see shadow. We were digging when the sun begin to die and our shadow come long. We were still digging when the sun don die finish and porson no fit see him brother again. And you know, all this time that we are digging, we no chop anything. Even to see water to drink we no see at all.

By the time wey night come, we don tire well well. So the soza captain after some time tell us make we fall for line again. Line for night? Oh, sozaman life no be small thing. So we entered for line and they begin march us left right, left right, through the bush until we near our house which is to me like school in Dukana. So they asked us to enter. Then they give us one one packet of biscuit. We ate that one quick quick because by now we are all very very hungry. And after that everybody put him waterproof for ground and lie down.

I was very happy to lie down. By this time small rain don begin dey fall, dey make noise for roof. I begin think of Agnes. But sleep catch me well well. I sleep.

LOMBER ELEVEN

When we wake up next morning, the rain was falling bad bad. The roof of the school was leaking plenty plenty and everywhere na soso water water. I was thinking to myself how are the pits that we dig last night. Water go don fill all well well. I was laughing small for my belly.

Then the soza captain came again. It is very early in the morning, oh. This soza captain is small man. I no think that the man fit old pass myself plenty. But always he is dressing very well. His uniform is very clean. And 'e dey wear him hat with style. Very thin man so. When he walk, na with speed like say porson dey pursue am. Him get three star for him shoulder. So as he came into that open place where we were sleeping, everybody begin to jump up because they know as this soza captain used to hala if porson is not doing something well. That is what happened yesterday when we were digging that pit wey water don full now. Many times the soza captain hala at some sozas. Then he give them punishment. Either they will make double quick march on one place or he will ask one sarzent to beat them. And if you see how the boys were crying ehn, you will sorry for them. So this morning, they are not looking for *wahala*. So immediately we all fall inside one line. Everybody attention. No movement.

So the soza captain say that he is very happy with what we have done yesterday. That we show that we learn the thing they teach us well well. That we will be good soza. That our job in that place that he called Iwoama is to stop the enemy from coming into that town. Because he will tief everything inside the town. Then he will take away all the women and begin to use them. And he will not stop at Iwoama. After Iwoama he will enter every place from Dukana and then he will go to Pitakwa. I beg oh, God no gree bad thing. Suppose as the soza captain come talk, enemy begin enter Iwoama? Then he will kill all of us plus myself. Then he will enter every place plus Dukana. Then they will carry away my mama plus Agnes and then begin to use Agnes. I beg, God no gree bad thing. Instead of that, we go fight sotey the world broke into two. No worry, soza captain, the enemy no go fit enter Iwoama. At all.

So the soza captain tell us that to stop the enemy, we must all work very hard and as him tell us yesterday, we must obey our leader. He said that sometime sef we will not get food to eat; no water to drink and no medicine, even if we sick. But we must not worry. Because everything will be awright after all. So this morning, he will give us new uniform and gun and he will divide us into three company. So he put myself and Bullet and thirty other boys in 'A' company. He said that Bullet is our leader. So he give am three ropes and another watch to wear for him hand. Like that for the three companies. Then he called those three people that he have made leader of the company and he begin to talk to them.

I was thinking to myself how I am lucky to be with Bullet in the same company. Because to talk true, I like am plenty. Na very fine man. And 'e sabi almost everything. And 'e no dey make *gra-gra*. All him things na *je-je*. And if you no know sometin and you aks am he will take time to explain to you. As he used to do his thing, you will think that that thing is easy to do, you will not know that it is very difficult. Because 'e get power to make big thing look like small easy thing. I was very happy to be in that 'A' company. I know that it will be very easy for me to obey Bullet. And I know that he will teach me all those things that I cannot understand. So that I will be very clever soza by the time we don finish the fighting.

Now, after the soza captain have spoken to the three new leaders that he called san mazor, he said *quashun* to all of us. We stopped talking or thinking. Then he told us again that now we all have san mazor – three of them. From this time, we must do what the san mazor say. Obey before complain. That is what the soza captain said. If there is trouble or disobedience, he will shoot all those who cause the trouble. Good morning. Then the soza captain turned and left.

That morning they gave all of us gun. Every porson one gun. It is the second time that I have hold gun in my own hand. And I am telling you I was very very proud of myself. New uniform plus gun. Even sef that gun dey wonder me plenty. I look am for him mouth. I look am for belly. I look am for bottom. Just small and thin. And with plenty of power. Short man bogey. I carry the gun for my hand. I put am down. I clean am small small. I pull him tooth, 'e talk small small. I come proud well well. And I dey laugh for myself. So now I be sozaboy proper proper. Wetin Zaza go talk now if 'e see me? I was thinking how I will take foto of myself inside new uniform with gun and then I will send the foto to Agnes and then she will show it to all those Dukana people. And they will be prouding when they know that one of their picken is now big soza. But I think that sometime I will wait small time so that I will get one rope or two rope or even three, then when I send the foto they will know that I no hold joke; that true true I am big man now in soza work.

Yes, that is what I will do. By that time sef, sometime I will even get bigger gun. But I like dis my new gun. It was even like the time that I first married Agnes. I was prouding plenty. And I see that the other sozas are also prouding plenty for their own gun. Everybody was looking at his gun like new wife dem just marry for am. But we no get plenty time to stay there that morning.

They ask us to fall into line again. And we begin to march. I am telling you, as we were marching today not as we used to march before. Everybody seem bigger than before; whether because of new uniform or because of gun, I do not know. But myself it is because of gun. I no look sef whether the gun is new or old. I am just proud of the gun when I remember that with that gun Chief Birabee go fall down for ground when he see me call me 'sah', 'Oga' and 'massa' and all those fine fine names.

It was still raining small small by this time and we were marching to that place where we dig pit yesterday. That is 'A' company with Bullet as sam mazor and 'our leader'. I no care for the rain sef. All I was remembering is what that soza captain tell us that we must work hard, obey our leader and not allow the enemy to formfool. I was saying to myself that if the enemy begin to formfool today that I have got gun, he will see pepper, red pepper. Ha! Ha!

By this time we have reached where we dig the pits yesterday. And true true water don enter am plenty. Then Bullet say that we must enter the pit two porson inside one pit. So he divided us into two two. Himself and myself were inside one pit. So I ask Bullet whether we shall remove the water first before we enter inside the pit. He shook his head. I no like this oh, but as they tell us to obey before complain, I cannot complain. And as other sozas were entering the pit, no complain, I myself did likewise. Bullet also entered the pit.

No sooner we enter that pit than I hear some thing. Yes, I hear something, some kain sound like dem shoot gun. I fear small. Then I was angry because I think it is one of our company who is shooting that gun. But Bullet tell me that it is not our boys who is shooting that gun. Then he pointed to the front. I look carefully. I cannot see anything at all. I wanted to get out of the pit so that I can see better still. So I was about to jump out when Bullet pushed me down. As he pushed me down, I hear another sound like gun and I see something like bird with sharp noise wey fly near my head.

"Careful, be careful," Bullet said.

"Whasmatter?" I asked.

"The enemy," Bullet answered. "The enemy is over there."

"Is it the enemy that is shooting?" I asked.

"Yes."

"So he have already begin to formfool wey day never broke and we get new gun for our hand."

"He was just greeting us."

"Is that the way to greet people for Iwoama?"

"That is a greeting at the front." And Bullet begin to laugh small small.

"If that is what this enemy go dey do, there will be plenty trouble," I said.

"Oh yes, there will be plenty trouble," said Bullet, and he

was laughing small small. After some time I begin to laugh too. After that day, nobody shoot again. But every day we must stay inside the pit. For evening time another Company will take our place. Or some time na we go stay for night time. All through the night. And porson no go sleep sef. Whether rain or no rain we dey stay inside the pit. The food wey dem give us for chop no too fine. In fact, dog no go fit chop dat kain chop. But as Bullet talk, war is war. Porson wey want better chop must wait until the war don finish.

"But which time de war go finish?" I asked Bullet.

"War will finish when everybody don die finish," he answered, and he begin laugh.

Look, I no like as Bullet dey take everything for joke. How war go finish when everybody don die finish? Na who go live to enjoy after that? Does it mean that myself, my wife Agnes and my mama go don die finish by that time? Then why are we fighting then?

As we are staying inside that pit, many things used to worry me you know. Like that question. Why are we fighting? I used to confuse plenty any time I ask that question to myself. I cannot ask Bullet because some time he will think that I am not doing what the soza captain said about obey before complain. So I just keep quiet so that they can give me one rope or two ropes. I am sure that as Bullet like me plenty he will soon give me rope. Only I want something to happen so that I can show them that I am good soza. Then they will give me rope. If I have that rope, then those Dukana people will know that I am not just Sozaboy but really tough man who can bring Hitla home.

But we waited plenty days. Nothing come happen. Then I remembered what that Chief Commander General was saying in big big grammar that day for the training camp – how he was saying that the enemy have tired and they cannot fight. If so, why do they not ask us to return to our home? So we continued to wait. And nothing happened. Everyday the same thing.

And something was very bad for that place, you know. Water to drink no dey. Common well sef, you cannot get. So that all the time, it was the water in the swamp that we were drinking. And that is also the place that we are going to latrine. Na the same water that we are bathing and using to wash some of our clothes. And na the same water we were using for cooking. That is if we get something to cook like eba and soup. But as you know, not every time that we can cook soup and eba. Even when we cook, na sozaman cook we dey cook. Just throw water, salt, pepper and small fish for pot at the same time. Otherwise, always small biscuit and tea for inside mess pan without sugar or anything. Christ Jesus, man picken don suffer well well.

All this time Bullet and myself we are like brothers. Because we are always staying in the same pit or we sleep near ourselves in the dormitory tent. I think this man likes me too much as me I like am too. We used to talk about everything. I told him how I was apprentice driver and then my mother and Agnes my new wife with J.J.C. And how Zaza and Bom, Terr Kole and Duzia are always talking things that will make porson laugh plenty. Bullet used to laugh plenty whenever I talk about Zaza and how he used to fight in Burma. I used to wonder why he was laughing like that. But when I asked him he will only laugh more and more. He told me how he too is the only son of his mother and father in Aba. How he have gone to school plenty and he can type letter and he have read plenty book. And he have now joined army because he knows that when the war don finish all those who have fight the war well will become big man. And he told me that as I am his brother now, when he becomes big man he must not forget me at all.

All these things made me very very happy and although we were suffering many bad things, I did not worry at all. Because bad thing must happen before good one come happen.

LOMBER TWELVE

One day, as we were inside the pit in the afternoon, I see something like handkerchief in the bush very far away. At first, I think that what I am seeing is not true. How can handkerchief grow in the bush? And white handkerchief too. I begin to think that I am stupid. But no. It is white handkerchief. And this handkerchief was going up, up, up. So I called Bullet and told him what I am seeing.

"What is the meaning of this handkerchief?" is what I asked Bullet.

"It means surrender," he answered. "That mean to say that the porson who is holding that handkerchief does not want to fight again. He want make we settle our quarrel. Make we talk. Make we no fight again."

"So true true that this enemy don tire for fight as the Chief Commander General was talking that day?" I asked.

"I no think so."

"You no think so? Are you saying that the Chief Commander General was telling lie that day to all of us? Is it?"

"I am not saying so. But sometimes, even the Chief Commander General, as you call him, can make mistakes. If he were correct, why should we be here today? And you remember the greeting we had when we first arrived here?"

As Bullet was speaking was confusing me again. I don't like how he used to talk big big grammar sometimes. Either he will be laughing small small and he will not talk plenty or if he wants to talk, he will make big big grammar and he will be confusing me. But the one that I am talking about now is not something to confuse about. Because true true that white handkerchief is moving nearer and nearer. So Bullet told me to go and tell everybody in their pit not to move at all. Not to shoot. But everybody must hold their gun ready. In case he gives them order to fire. So I jumped from our own pit and went to all the other pits and told them as Bullet have said and then quick quick I come return to my own pit. So I no go miss anything that the white handkerchief will do.

"Now, you hold your gun on the ready. Release the safety catch and keep your hand on the trigger. Keep cool. And keep your mouth shut."

If na before I will not understand what Bullet is saying but, you know, sitting in this pit for one month, I am beginning to know one or two things. Even the big big grammar that used to confuse me proper proper before no dey confuse me too much again. Even, I can speak some big grammar sometimes myself. Just I will repeat what Bullet or the soza captain have said. And I will say it carefully with my mouth and with style so that if you hear me talking by that time, you will even think that I am oyibo man. Even Bullet come give me one book and every time when I get small chance I will try to read the book. It was very tough for me, I am telling you, but if there is some word I do not know, I must ask Bullet and he will explain to me. I was prouding of myself plenty.

The white handkerchief that is moving is not a thing for joke at all. So I have heard what Bullet said about being ready. And I must not talk at all. Now the white handkerchief begin to near us. I can see that no be just handkerchief wey dey move by itself. 'E get man wey dey hold the handkerchief. But 'e no dey show himself. Just dey go on him belly, small small. So by this time, Bullet come hold handkerchief by himself. So that the porson who is coming will know that everything is awright. So when the man see Bullet's handkerchief, he stood up and begin to walk to where we are. Him put two hands up to show that he have no gun. So when Bullet see that the man no hold gun, he jumped out of the pit. But he looked at me as if to say 'I think you remember what I told you before'.

Bullet stood attention. And when the man came near, they

shook hands together. So the man bring out a packet of cigarette and gave Bullet one stick. Bullet took it and they begin to smoke. So the man said that the two of them should sit down. Then they sat down together. At first, they cannot talk easily because as you know, they do not know what to talk about. But the man come bring one bottle of *ginkana* from him pocket and he drank it first. Then he gave it to Bullet. That one drink too. Straight from the bottle. Then the man laugh small small. Then Bullet begin laugh too, small small.

All this time my finger dey for the trigger. I never fire gun before as you know. And I don't know as it will be if I pull that trigger. I am wondering to myself; but I also like as the man dey drink dey pass the bottle to Bullet. They drink like that until the drink finish well well. So the man bring another bottle. 'E tell Bullet make him give some to him friends wey dey inside 'those cold trenches' as him talk am. Na pit de man dey call 'trench' you know. Sometime 'e don drink proper no remember de correct name again.

"I will see you again tomorrow." That is what he said before he begin to crawl for belly return to the place that he have commot from. When he reach far far place, Bullet told me to return the catch of my rifle. He gave me the bottle of *ginkana* that the soza have left behind.

I drank it small small. Then Bullet said that I should send it to the next pit, make the other sozas drink too and pass until everybody have drunk. So that night every soza drank small *ginkana* and the pit was not too cold for us. And we were very happy because since we reach that place, we have never see any hot drink. Only tea for bag and the water no dey hot sef.

But there was something which was worrying me for mind. I think I have seen that man before. I sure say I have seen that sozaman before. Oh God, where I have seen that sozaman before? That tall man with plenty tooth. Where have I see him before? I asked Bullet whether he have seen the man before. 'E say him never see am from Adam. So I ask am why de man come. And why 'e bring drink. And whether true true na dis man dem dey call enemy.

"Oh yes. That man is the enemy," Bullet replied. "Look, Sozaboy, we are in war front, o.k. And in the war front, there are all sorts of people. Drunkards, thieves, idiots, wise men, foolish men. There is only one thing which binds them all. Death. And everyday they live, they are cheating death. That man came to celebrate the fact."

"Bullet," I said, "I beg you, no make too much grammar for me. I beg you. Try talk the one that I will understand. No vex because I ask you this simple question."

"No, I no dey vex," Bullet replied after some time. "I no dey vex. What I am saying is that all of us who are here can die any time. Any time. So while we live, we must drink. Because, as you know, man must wak." This Bullet is very clever man you know. Man must wak. I like that. Man must wak.

So throughout that night, I was just thinking of the tall man and where I have meet him before and the *ginkana* that was inside my head and making my body hot and how Bullet say that man must wak. It was like that till day broke and we return to the dormitory barrack.

So now, the whole of that day, I no fit sleep or do anything at all. If Bullet no be porson wey like me, I for enter inside pepper soup proper. Because 'e no get anything that I do well. I was just thinking of that tall man and *ginkana* and man must wak. Even I begin to call the man 'Manmuswak'. So, I told Bullet that we shall call the man Manmuswak. 'E say the name is very good for the man. And he think that the man must like the name when we tell am. Then I ask 'am if he think that the man will come back again.

"Yes, I think so," Bullet replied. So indeed I was very happy at all when I heard that the man will be coming back. That afternoon I hurried quick and went to the pit. Bullet was there and the other boys too. I waited throughout that afternoon and the man did not come. I waited in the night and the man did not come. Every time I will be asking Bullet what is the time. And always I am thinking that the man must come before midnight or latest for midnight. But the man did not come. He did not come for three nights and, I am telling you, this thing was beginning to pain me too much. Why is the man doing this kain thing to me? Ehn? Why? Look, I was very surprised myself how I was wanting to see the man. Was it long throat for his *ginkana* or is it because I think I have seen the man before for some place and I cannot remember where I have seen the man? So I tried not to show the other sozas especially Bullet that I am not happy that Manmuswak have not come. I tried but I no fit. Anyway, he came on the fourth night.

It was evening time that I saw white handkerchief and told Bullet immediately. "Oga, Manmuswak dey come oh." So immediately everybody was looking in the same place where Manmuswak will come. The white handkerchief begin move small small, small small until 'e near us. Then 'e stop. Then Bullet bring out his own handkerchief. Then the man bring down white handkerchief, stand up and then begin to walk to where we were inside the pit. Bullet jump commot go meet am. This time he no tell me anything about cock rifle or no cock rifle. 'E dey me like say he was wanting to see that man quick quick like myself too. So Manmuswak come and he began to smoke cigar. 'E give Bullet one cigar box. Then he gave me one box make me and the other sozas take one one. We all begin smoke immediately. Because since we reach that Iwoama we never smoke at all. Nobody fit think that we can smoke sef. I hear de time wey Manmuswak dey ask Bullet whether we no get cigarette ration.

"At all, at all," was what Bullet answered.

"I am sure you people have cigarette ration. But maybe na your Commanding Officer dey use all by himself," Manmuswak said.

This talk confuse Bullet small as I see. So he refuse to reply anything. Sometime he is thinking about it as I am turning the thing for my mind. So, that soza captain fit dey use cigarette wey be for the soza for himself? Na so to fight the enemy? Soza go dey work and soza captain go dey chop. Anyway, I lef dat one small. I go think am another time.

"Do you people chop three times every day?"

"No." Bullet replied.

"Well, we chop three times every day. And the chop is very very good. Why una no dey chop well? Una go fit fight when war begin?" And 'e begin laugh one small laugh. "Whosai dem dey keep una chop? *Abi* your Commanding Officer dey chop all the food by himself?" asked Manmuswak.

Ha! the soza captain is chopping all the food by himself? If this thing is true something go bad for everybody oh.

So that night, Manmuswak did not spend long time with us. After some time he told us that we must to be careful because nobody can know when the war will come reach our front. So we told him goodnight, and he began to go away, small small like tall snake passing through the bush, making small noise.

LOMBER THIRTEEN

So now after Manmuswak have gone and we have all smoke the cigar which he give us, all that confusion began in my mind again. Because I cannot understand why Manmuswak who is enemy is coming to give us drink and cigar and is talking to us like our brother. Is that how to fight for war? If Hitla was like that, why did they follow him in Burma forest? Or is this Manmuswak ghost or spirit or juju? No. He cannot be ghost or spirit or juju. Because I have seen that tall man before. But na where I see am, oh God? Where?

"In the captain's tent," Bullet said.

"De soza captain tent, Bullet?"

"Yes."

"Impossible?"

"What's impossible?"

"No be for de soza captain tent wey I see am."

"See who?"

"Dis Manmuswak. No."

"Are you dreaming? I was telling you where the drinks and the cigarettes are."

"Oh, you are thinking of drink and cigar?"

"Yes. And what were you thinking of?"

"I am thinking where I have seen this Manmuswak before."

"Okay. You can continue thinking of that. I'm dropping out with one or two of the boys. You stay here and keep a bright lookout. I'll soon be back," Bullet said.

Ha! Trouble no dey ring bell. He have never done this type of thing before. Where is he going now? And this Manmuswak, where I have seen him before? So I was thinking about these things for long long time. Then I just remember. Yes. I have seen Manmuswak before. At the African Upwine Bar in New York, Diobu. That night when Agnes told me that she come from Dukana. Oh yes. It is this Manmuswak who was saying that he will fight as dem tell am to fight. He is the man who was chopping *ngwo-ngwo* and drinking *tombo* with that short man. Yes! This Manmuswak is the same tall man! So he is the enemy now. And I was thinking how this man come join the enemy? Haba. My confusion have start again. And as I was turning this thing for my mind, I come remember my Agnes and my mama. So what are they doing now? Do they know that I am sitting here inside pit smoking cigar in Iwoama with frog singing and plenty of dirty water everywhere and bush and forest, and night and darkness? Does my darling Agnes know that I am thinking of her now? Or *abi* have she run away with another man because she have wait for me tire and I do not return? So I said "God no gree bad thing." Agnes cannot be able to forget me like that. Even if she want to forget me, my mama will not allow her because my mama must to take her like her own picken. That is what I was thinking to myself. And I was thinking that whether whether, one day I will return to Dukana and I will meet my Agnes and my mama. And my mother will be happy. And my Agnes will be prouding because her husband is soza proper proper who have fought and conquered the enemy and have allowed plenty of salt to enter Dukana after all said and done.

And I was thinking too how Zaza and Duzia and Terr Kole will not be laughing at me again and when they see me they will run because I am very strong soza. And sometimes I will get one or two ropes or even I can be soza captain as something used to be. And when the war ends, I will be very big man. Sometimes they can even make me the chief of Dukana instead of that stupid man, Chief Birabee, who is always fearing and shaking whenever he see any soza captain or even sozaman. And if I am soza captain, I will be smoking plenty cigar and drinking plenty *ginkana*. So when I think of cigar and *ginkana* and the soza captain, I come remember that Bullet is not inside the pit again and since he went away he have not returned. Where did he go? And he have never commot from the pit since we reach this Iwoama. Except this night. And now he have stayed too long. I begin fear because he have taken away some of the soza boys and now plenty people are not inside that pit again. Suppose enemy come now will they not take hand catch me? Na me one go fit stay here fight them? I think I will go and look for Bullet. Yes, I must go look for him so that he will come stay for the pit with me. But where will I look for him? Or *abi*? Because he told me that I must stay in the pit and keep bright lookout. That is exactly what he said. But I was fearing that some time something bad have happened to him. So I said I must go and look for him true true. So I keep my gun inside the pit and I begin move small small inside that darkness to go and look for Bullet.

It was very dark and even small small rain was beginning to fall. I was shaking inside the uniform as I was walking slowly slowly inside that night. Lucky enough, I have not gone far when one man come catch me from the back. The man come wrestle me till I fall down. And as you know, I cannot shout because of fear that I will wake everybody. Thank God it was Bullet. So he told me in soft voice how I am foolish. I told him that I was going to look for him. So he said how can I look for him when I do not know where he have gone? And he does not like me because I have disobeyed him. And suppose the enemy come that time when I am not in the pit and he himself is not there, what will happen? So I tell him that I am sorry. And I asked where he went. So he asked me to follow him back to the pit. When we got there, I see plenty of bottles of drink and plenty of cigar. He told me that he went to the soza captain tent. And the soza captain was sleeping well well with one young girl. And na true what that Manmuswak was saying, because all the hot drink and cigar which the Chief Commander General told him to give all the sozas, he have been drinking and smoking by himself. And he is sleeping with women every day. Drinking and smoking and sleeping with woman. And we are here inside pit and the rain is beating us every night and no hot drink or cigar for us. So Bullet said that he does not like that type of thing. And I said that I agree with him. That it is good thing that he have gone to that soza captain tent to bring the hot drink and the cigar. He said I should go and call all the boys from the pit, so that we will all smoke and drink together so that cold will not catch us because of the rain. So I went and called all the boys. Everybody was very happy when they saw so many bottles of hot drink and plenty boxes of cigar. I am telling you I have not seen such thing before. Every soza was holding one bottle of drink in one hand and cigar in another hand. And we were drinking and smoking, drinking and smoking for very long time. By this time all our guns were inside pit. We just forget everything about guard and fight and war or no war. We were just jollying because it is the first time we have seen so much drink. And after, everybody was saying that Bullet is very good soza. And in fact, that he is the right porson to be our captain because if he is the soza captain then drink and cigar will flow like water and all the sozas will be very happy. After now, as the drink come enter we body we begin to sing and dance. We were singing and dancing like that until we all become very tired and then some of the sozas just lie down there begin to sleep like stupid goat.

I will not tell you a lie. Because lie is not a good thing. When I opened my eyes, day have broke well well. And we were not near the pit at all. We were inside one place they used to call Kampala. If you know as this Kampala dey, you will sorry for me when I tell you that we were inside Kampala. Both Bullet and myself and all the boys. This Kampala is like hell. Anybody who goes inside there cannot return the same as before. I think you understand. This Kampala is the worst prison that anybody can go inside. The floor is the bed . The floor is the latrine. The floor is everything. And you will stay in that tent without water and no food. And then they just barb your head *mala*. No single hair at all. Then one san mazor will come every time and call all of you out and you will mark time, left right, left right, left right for up to four hours. And if you just stop for even one minute, he will use the *koboko* and beat you until you piss and shit. And you will call your mother and you cannot see her. And you will call your God and there is no God. And every time the san mazor will continue to shout: "You anmals. You think soza work na picken work. You think war front na hotel bar. God don punish all of you today. When una finish for dis Kampala, una go remember de day wey una mama born una. Anmals."

Then the san mazor will bring out his *koboko* and give every porson twenty-four. Like that for seven days. And it is not only marking time and beating with *koboko*, oh. If na so, I no for talk. But we just dey dig pit, big big pit. Carry sand-sand. All the dirty work in war front. And no food and no drink. One day the san mazor come tie me and Bullet for hand and he beat us as the soza captain tell am till we no fit cry again. I think that he want to kill us sef. God no gree bad thing. I thank God as I did not die in that Kampala.

After the seven days have finish, they first tell us to go and see the soza captain. So the soza captain looked at our body well well, and he saw as all our eyes have gone inside and all our tongue have dry. Then the soza captain laughed. He laughed till he begin to cry. Then he told us that we are bloody stupid bastards. He ask whether we want drink hot and smoke again. We could not answer him even. That one make him more angry still.

"So una no wan smoke and drink hot again? Una no go come for my tent for night come tief my drink and cigar? You bastard *ashewo* Bullet. I think you are the ring leader. I will show you pepper today."

Then the soza captain opened one bottle and give it to Bullet to drink. So Bullet who have thirsty quench just took that bottle for him hand put the drink for him mouth. Look, I am telling you that what I see that day, I can never forget it until I die. Because I was looking at Bullet face as he drank that drink. And his face was the face of porson who have already dead. And when he finished the bottle, the soza captain begin laugh and the san mazor laugh too. Then they asked us to get out. Bullet no fit walk by himself. Na we hold am. I think that he must die. God no gree bad thing.

For almost two weeks, Bullet refused to talk to anybody. Even if you greet him like you are his friend, he will not talk to you. This thing begin fear me. Because I always like him before. I like as he is quiet gentleman dey knack big big grammar. Dey laugh small small. But as I saw him after that Kampala, I think wickedness enter for him body. I saw it in his eye. Because they have removed all the ropes that he have. He is not san mazor, not sarzent, not corple not even one rope. I was sorry for him.

One night, when everybody have sleep, he just call me softly: "Sozaboy." I open my eye small small.

"Sozaboy."

"Oga, Bullet."

"You know that day after we return from Kampala go the captain tent?"

I say yes I know. How porson go fit forget?

"You know the thing that man give me to drink?"

I tell Bullet that I do not know. And true true I no know.

"Na urine."

"Urine!"

"Yes. One bottle of urine! No tell anybody oh. This na war front. But I will tell you because I like you. Na that captain and myself for this war front. One day na one day."

That was all Bullet said. Then he turned his face away. I think he was crying small small. Because I can hear his body shaking. My brother, I cannot tell you what I was thinking that night. I see for my mind eye as the soza captain was urinating into the bottle and as he gave the bottle to Bullet. I see as Bullet closed his eye to drink that bottle of urine. I see as the soza captain was laughing. I see Manmuswak with him white handkerchief. I see all these things. And I see other things. And I know that there will be trouble. Trouble will bring trouble. And trouble does not ring bell.

And I fall asleep.

LOMBER FOURTEEN

T rue true, trouble does not ring bell. Since we return from Kampala, Bullet and myself are not staying inside pit again. The soza captain say we are more useless than shit. We did not mind that one because to stay inside it is to suffer proper proper. But what happened was even more than. Because the soza captain begin to send us on patrol. As petrol burns, that is how this patrol kills. Quick quick. That is what Bullet told me. He said that although many of the sozas are dying every time they go on patrol, you can never see their dead body because they will always bury them before they return to the Camp. So when I hear that I will start to go on patrol, I know immediately that water don pass gari. Water don pass gari.

I think you know as I was thinking when I entered army the first time and wear sozaman uniform. You remember as I was prouding because now Zaza and Terr Kole will not be laughing at me because they think I am not good man and strong, the only thing I can do is to stay at home and marry J.J.C. And you know as I was prouding when they give us gun the first time and I think I can even go and bring Hitla from Burma. Well, I am telling you now that something come spoil my mind small. Yes. Because since Manmuswak come tell us about cigar for soza captain tent and we come go Kampala and since that time na soso work work work, I begin see as Tan Papa was saying before, that true true, war is war. I know because I can see what *koboko* have done to my back. I know because I know what to stand for pit for one night mean. I know because I see Bullet face as he drank urine from that bottle. War is war. And now I have to go on patrol. And when I think of that patrol, it is not Zaza with his loin cloth for Dukana talking about Hitla and Burma that I see. It is not my mama and my Agnes that I see. It is not Duzia who have no legs that I see. It is my Papa that have died long time that I see. He always appear to me in day time and at night. I think that the man is laughing me. And I tell you, I begin fear small small. Since I join soza, I have not know what they call fear. When I saw that sozaman running when he saw water that time when we have just reach this Iwoama, I think you remember how I was laughing and cursing the man. I was cursing the man because of his fear. By that time, I do not know what is fear. But I think I have begin to know it now. Small small. Small small.

But you know I cannot allow myself to show this fear. Even I just drive it from my mind. I said to myself that Sozaboy cannot fear anything. Because I must return to my Agnes and my mama with plenty rope. Oh yes. And I can only get this rope if we go on patrol and I show that I am big Sozaboy.

So one early morning they woke myself and Bullet and other boys very early and said that we must go on patrol in canoe. So we packed up all our things and entered the canoe quick quick, no waste time. Day have not break well well but we can see ourselves. The soza captain tell us that our work is to see what the enemy is doing, and make sure that he does not try to move from where he is to come and attack us. And if we see him, we should fight him and if he is too strong, we should return to tell the soza captain.

So now we begin paddle the canoe small small through the swamp and creek. By the time we get to the river, day have break well well. We still paddle the canoe. Bullet say we must to be careful because plenty of our sozas have already dead in this patrol business. We did not go too far. We saw no any enemy at all. But we hear gun shooting from far. When they shoot, the bullet will land inside the water. One time, the bullet just pass over my head. *Heeeuun! Heeeuun!* I just fall inside the canoe. So I ask Bullet what all this nonsense mean. So he said that the enemy is also on patrol. And if he can shoot and kill us, he will shoot and kill us. And if we can shoot and kill them, we too must to do so. When I hear of shoot and kill, fear begin catch me small. Then I said to myself that nobody can kill me because I must return to Dukana with plenty rope. Then the enemy begin to shoot again. And Bullet return the fire. He fire them many times. He fire till he no get fire for inside him gun. Then the other boys begin to fire too. They fire plenty. But I myself, I was only looking at them like *mumu*, I did not even fire one time. My hand just no want move. So as all the fire have finished, we just turn the canoe, return to the camp.

When we reach the camp now, the soza captain begin hala for us. He say we return too quick. So Bullet told him that we return because we do not get fire inside our gun again. The soza captain say we just waste ammo. I never hear that word before. I was just wondering what he mean by this ammo. The soza captain said that good good soza cannot waste ammo because ammo is for soza as water is for fish. Because if fish have no water, it will die. And if soza have no ammo, that soza is dead body proper. Bullet told him that we are not wasting ammo only the enemy was too plenty in the place that we went. So the soza captain said he does not believe what Bullet is talking because he is big liar. And stupid tief. As he talked this one, I can see as Bullet is biting his lips like say he remembered the bottle of urine that the captain have give him to drink before before. Then the soza captain said that he will go and see for himself exactly what is happening. He asked us to get the speed boat ready and together we will go to see whether Bullet is talking true or talking lie. And he told Bullet that if he is talking lie, he will send him to Kampala for two weeks. Again I see as Bullet bite his lips. I think that if he is not strong man, he will even have cried.

We begin put the ammo box inside the speed boat. And Bullet and myself and the other boys begin to load our gun. When we finish, we all march one by one to the water and we entered the speed boat. We were waiting there for a long time because the soza captain did not leave his tent quick. As we were waiting now, Bullet called me.

"Sozaboy," he said.

"Yes, Oga."

"Something must happen today, Sozaboy."

"Whasmatter?" is what I asked.

"'E dey me for body like something go happen," he replied. "And when that thing happen, I want you to help me. I think you understand?" So I told him that I have understand. That I will help him whether whether because I like him and he is even like my brother.

All the other boys – four of them – were sitting like *mumu* inside the speed boat. Not that they cannot talk or do something but you know as this soza life dey. You cannot talk or do as you like. Every time you must follow your leader like goat. And all of us come like Bullet because the man is gentleman. And since that day that he have went to the soza captain tent to bring cigar and drink which made them send all of us to Kampala and give him urine to drink, all the sozas were not happy with the soza captain. But they don't know what to do because Bullet himself said nothing. Even the boys do not know that it is urine that the soza captain gave him to drink. Na me one wey 'e tell. But all the boys are sympathising with him. And although the soza captain removed him from san mazor and took away all his ropes, all the boys still respect him and they will do anything that he tell them to do. So when the new san mazor is there, they will all keep quiet and you will think they are *mumu*. But if Bullet talk to them, they will do exactly as he tell them. Even sef, they cannot respect the soza captain as they respect Bullet.

Then the soza captain begin to march from his tent to where we were all sitting in the speed boat. Before he reach where we were staying, Bullet turned to the boys who were sitting like *mumu* and said "No be everything wey eye see that mouth dey talk. I think una understand?"

All the boys together answer "Ya" and then they continue to sit like *mumu*. By this time the soza captain have reached the speed boat. Then he entered the boat, sat down, and gave order for the boat to move. The boat man start the engine and the boat just shoot for front quick quick with plenty noise. We passed the mangrove swamp, bend through the creek with plenty mudskippers and crabs and the birds singing in the tree. Soon, we come reach the river. As soon as we reach the river, the enemy begin shoot for the water. Shoot, shoot, shoot. But the bullet did not reach our boat. So the soza captain asked everybody to get their gun ready and begin to shoot the enemy.

As they were shooting, the soza captain put one big spectacle in his eye. I think they call it binocular as Bullet tell me. With this binocular, the soza captain can see everything that is happening very very far away. The soza captain continued to look through his binocular. He did not see what I saw. And what I saw is this: Bullet get up from where he was sitting in front of the soza captain, turned round quickly, aimed his gun at the soza captain and just shoot. The soza captain do like say he wants to stand up and Bullet push him immediately so that the soza captain fall straight into the river. Then Bullet shoot him again. By this time, all the boys stopped shooting the enemy. All of them just stand up. The engine just stop too and the boat no move again. Then Bullet keep down his gun and carried up his two hands like to say 'I surrender'. He kept his hands like this for a long time before he said "If anybody no like what I have done, that porson fit shoot me." All the boys just keep quiet. Then he said: "You will all remember what I said before. It is not everything that your eye see that your mouth will talk. Come on, Sozaboy, help me carry that anmal into the boat."

Bullet jumped into the river and begin to swim to where the soza captain body was floating in the river. I too jumped inside follow am. So we carry the soza captain body put for the speed boat. All our cloth and body were wet well well. The soza captain don die one time. Then we turn the speed boat round and begin return to the camp.

All of us were sitting in the speed boat like mumu. Nobody talked. Only the engine of the speed boat was making plenty noise like he was crying. The river gave us plenty trouble with big waves because the wind was blowing like no man business. We tried to leave that troublesome river.

Soon, we reached the mangrove swamp. The waves did not disturb us again. By this time the water have full the mangrove. No mudskipper or crab again. Even the birds for the tree did not sing again. Throughout that time, I saw only one vulture for one tree. As if he knew that dead body was inside the boat, he began to follow us as we were moving through the creeks to the camp. The soza captain body was in the bottom of the boat. I

look am well. His eye still open as if he have not already d
tell you, fear begin catch me small small. I did not know
the other boys were thinking because they all sit in the
boat like *mumu*. I looked at Bullet. Bullet looked at me. E no
dey Bullet like anything happen as I see for him eye. But that
wickedness wey I dey see for him eye don disappear. Even 'e
dey me like say 'e happy. But you no go see happiness for him
face. Only for him eye.

After some time, we reached the camp. Bullet was the first to
jump from the boat. He went quickly to tell the new san mazor
that enemy have killed the soza captain. He told him that the
soza captain is inside the boat. I see as the new san mazor look
Bullet for eye. Then he begin to walk quick quick to the boat.
So when he reached the boat, he saw the soza captain body. So
he salute the dead body well well. He ask all of us to *qua shun* and
present arms. We stay like that for about two minutes. Then he
asked us to *ajuwaya* and fall out and carry the dead body to the
soza captain tent.

We all join to carry the dead body to the soza captain tent.
We keep him there and we all went away to our tent to change
our uniform which was wet. As we were changing uniform I
can hear the san mazor saying that soza man life is *ye–ye*. Every
soza is dead body. That's what the new san mazor talk.

If I tell you I was happy, know that I am telling a lie.

LOMBER FIFTEEN

No sooner we have changed our uniform than I hear the sound of aeroplane in the sky. I am telling you since I came to this war front we have never seen the plane whether in the night or in the day. And you know as we used to look up every time when the plane pass because it is a very wonderful thing to see this canoe sailing in the sky through the air. Every time we see the plane, we used to say "Chei, Oyibo don try," because it is very very surprising how they are able to do this thing. So, when we see the plane for up, we all run go look it. This plane passed our camp many times, just going round and round and still we do not know what is happening. I think that if the soza captain was alive, he will have known what is the meaning of the plane, and he for tell us what we have to do. But the soza captain don die like goat and now only the new san mazor is in charge of the camp.

So as we were still looking at the plane as it came to pass round and round the camp, I saw that plane drop something. 'E dey me like say the plane dey shit and I begin laugh. But my laugh no reach my belly because that thing from the plane just land near we camp and I hear very very big noise which come carry me for air throway for ground. Then I hear Bullet shouting "Bomb! bomb! Take cover! Take cover!"

My dear brother, you have not seen the type of confusion that I see that morning. Everybody in that camp was running up and down. Nobody know what to do. The plane still was making noise for the sky. Going round and round our camp. Then it will drop bomb. Then I hear another big sound like one thousand palm tree dey fall for ground all at once. As soon as that big sound stop, I can hear some sozas crying and crying to God, to them mama and papa. Ha! Trouble no dey ring bell. Na so throughout that morning. I no see Bullet again. Only that time when he was shouting 'Bomb! bomb! Take cover!' Then I see something like fire for the place where he was running and I did not see him again.

Afterwards the plane just disappear. I did not see it again and I did not hear the noise. I think it was about ten minutes from the time it started, but true true I myself thought it was about three or four hours.

After the plane have disappeared, then I got up from where I was hiding. Oh Jesus Christ son of God, the thing wey I see my mouth no fit talk am. Oh God our father wey dey for up, why you make man wicked like this to his own brother? Oh Mary, mother of Jesus, pray for us to God to forgive us all our sins and not to kill us like fly because of our wickedness. Angel Gabriel, please beg God if he does not want us to live, make 'e no make us only to kill us after like goat or rat or rabbit. Oh, I can never never forget what I saw that morning.

All our camp don broke down well well. Everywhere was full of pit and pit and pit. And inside one pit, you will see the head of soza, and in another pit, the leg of soza and in another pit, the hand of soza. Everywhere, soso human flesh in small small pieces! Finger, nail, hair, *prick*, *blokkus*. Oh, I just begin cry like woman. Oh, foolish man, na who send me make I go join soza? Then I just remember say I never see Bullet. My heart just cut one time. *Abi* Bullet don die? Ehn? God, whosai 'e dey? I begin run about dey hala well well, 'Bullet, Oga Bullet, Bullet where you dey?' I look everywhere. 'E no dey. All de sozas wey no die or no wound join me begin dey look for Bullet. So we come to one pit and I see one hand with watch dey stretch from inside de pit. I know say na Bullet watch be dat one. So, me and one soza begin pull de hand sotey we pull Bullet from de pit. I see say 'e don die. The bomb just make grave for am one time. So I just cover my friend up. Then I kneel down there begin cry like woman. I see say my best friend for dis war front don die. And I know say my life don begin spoil small small. Before dis time, I no know wetin to die mean. All my life just sweet dreams. Now, today today, I don see say life no be as I dey see am before. I know say wickedness plenty. And I know say my life must change one time.

I think you understand as that camp dey that day. The soza captain don die. The san mazor don die. Bullet don die. Many of the sozamen don die. Na just few of us remain. Young young boys wey no know anything about war. Some of us never see dead body before. And we no know what is bomb or that aeroplane dey shit bomb wey dey kill. And just that morning we see death. We all confuse. We no know wetin to do. And like say something never bad reach, we begin dey hear gun dey shoot. This gun wey dey shoot no be like other guns you know. You can hear it from more than twenty miles. And when the bullet fall for the camp, it will be like bomb from aeroplane. As those guns were shooting, I know that it is better just to stay where I am because person fit run go die as him no for die if he stay one place. After some time, they stop shooting that heavy gun. Then the small gun start shooting. I look up and I see that the enemy is coming nearer and nearer. I remember as Tan Papa tell me one night. That if soza want to make heavy attack, first he must use mortar to give wetin they call covering fire as the sozas are moving small small. Then the sozas will just enter the enemy camp. And they will shoot and kill. And anybody that they do not kill, if they catch him they will take him to make prisoner of war.

This prisoner of war palaver, I no like it at all. Because Tan Papa don tell me that any soza wey become prisoner him life wor-wor pass slave. He will be carrying shit, and they will beat him; he will dig pit and they will slap him. In short, it is better to die one time than to be prisoner of war.

So as I see those enemy sozas coming near our camp, I just beg God make him help me. I remove my soza uniform, remain just my knicker and I begin run. I run zig-zag. I run and hide behind tree. I run I no know where I am going. I run for swamp sotey that dirty water reach me for mouth. I swim like fish. Then I enter inside forest. The weeds catch my leg and I fall. Blood just commot from all my body. Still I do not mind. All I want to do is to run away from those enemy sozas. I can never never be prisoner of war. I no mind whether tiger or snake or leopard or any dangerous anmal is in the forest where I was running. I does not care. I does not know even where I am running to even, whether forward or backward. I no think say fear allowed me to think anything at all. And I does not know whether day have break or night come fall. Because for inside that forest, night and day na one. I was running until my leg cannot carry me again. And then I just stopped under one big tree and just die.

I don't know how long I die. But I think I die for very very long time. When I wake up, I no fit carry up my hand sef. All my leg heavy like say dem take heavy thing put on top. I look my body and I no think say na my own body. I am sure that my face go don swell like pawpaw. So I begin sorry for myself. I begin cry. I remember as Zaza was talking in Dukana that day about Hitla and no Hitla for Burma. I remember as I come take money from my mama go bribe Mr. Okpara so that he will put me in the Army. I remember as I was prouding for my young wife Agnes. I remember as I was thinking that to be soza is a very good thing. I remember all the big big grammar that the Chief Commander General was telling us that day in Pitakwa. And I remember as Tan Papa was telling me that war is war. I remember as when we get to that Iwoama this Manmuswak begin come tell us about cigar and drink. I say to myself that if Manmuswak did not come to tell us that the soza captain is cheating us, that Bullet will not go to the soza captain tent to bring the drink. Then we will not have go to Kampala and the soza captain will not have give Bullet urine to drink and Bullet will not have killed the soza captain. And if the soza captain did not die that morning when the plane come, he will have told us what to do and even talk inside him tent to the radio to those big big men in Pitakwa and then all the sozas will not have died like rat as they die that day.

I just think that that Manmuswak is proper cunny man. Na him come confuse all of us. Na him come spoil the war. And now all my friends don die or sometimes Manmuswak don take some of them make prisoner of war. And I come say to myself that oh my God, war is very bad thing. War is to drink urine, to die and all that uniform that they are giving us to wear is just to deceive us. And anybody who think that uniform is fine thing is stupid man who does not know what is good or bad or not good at all or very bad at all. All those things that they have been telling us before is just stupid lie. All that one that Zaza is talking about is not true at all. Zaza have not gone to any Burma to fight any Hitla. He have not married any white woman at all. Sometime Zaza is just like myself wey dem drive to the war front like *mumu* goat who does not know where he is going. Sometimes he is just like myself who will only obey and do anything that he is told. Oh yes, that is how Zaza is. And all that thing he is talking about big big fight in Burma is one stupid lie. And na that Zaza come confuse me make me to leave Dukana come suffer for this swamp for Iwoama. Even, I no understand what I was doing until now. I come begin see as I dey think for that swamp that day that true true I do not know why we are fighting the war. The Chief Commander General have not told us why we are fighting. No. Tan Papa did not tell us why we are fighting. The soza captain did not tell us why we must go inside the pit. I just carry gun, fight, go inside pit because they tell me to carry gun, fight, go inside pit; right turn, left turn, about turn, udad arms, run, no run, stand still, chop, piss, shit. Every thing they tell me, I must do, no question.

This is what I was thinking as I was inside that forest. That day, no food and no water to drink and all my body with plenty wound and my leg big like elephant body and headache dey worry me and I no fit carry up my hand. So I come remember that dream that I was dreaming in Dukana before the fight proper come begin. How I was running away from the sozas who were pursuing me because I do not want to be soza.

Then I come remember how my mama was telling me how she come dream about plane that was flying over the Church and spoiling many things. So when I remember that one, I begin to think of my mama and Agnes. I know that if this trouble come reach Dukana and bomb begin fall from plane, then either all Dukana people go die and my mama and young wife will die or they are hiding in forest like myself without water and food and nothing to cure their wound. So I said impossible. I cannot be alive and my mama and my young wife Agnes will be suffering. Even sef I come remember as that thick man was saying in the church that day about the salt and no salt in our salt and in our body. And I know that I must return immediately to Dukana whether I strong or I no strong. I get wound or I no get wound. Because if true true that this trouble have reached Dukana, then something will be very bad for me.

So I begin to pick myself one by one. My hand, then my leg. I just sit down begin think how I will get to Dukana. No money for my hand; no cloth for my body only one short knicker. And even sef I no know the road.

But first as my body weak, I know that I must find some small wackies otherwise I cannot move one step. And my brother, if I tell you that I begin chop fresh snail make you no surprise. The water I dey drink na the dew wey settle for leaf for early morning. Then sometime I will find the root of cassava. I will chop it just like that. Then I find plenty fruit. Some I never see before, but hungry will just make me pluck them and begin to chop. So I was plucking and eating the fruits like that plus snails and other anmals for long long time. And although my body was still paining me and I cannot move my feet and my hands unless with pain, I begin to think more and more of my mama and Agnes. And I know I must go back to Dukana to look for them.

The forest no gree porson know when day don break or otherwise. But whether whether I must reach Dukana and I know that that Iwoama is not far from Pitakwa because that day when they carried us in the lorry to that war front we did not stay long time in the lorry. So I begin to pray to God that if he like my mama and my wife Agnes and he want me to see them again he must help me to reach Dukana. So I know that I must return to Dukana quick quick whether I well or I no well. So I begin to think that it will better for me if I travel in the night because in the daytime I can fit see the enemy and even sef if farmer or fisherman or any woman come see me inside my knicker and no shirt and plenty wound for my body and I no fat, they can take me to make prisoner of war again. Or they will think that I am ghost or juju or mad man and they can do me some bad thing. But I know that first of all I must leave that forest quick quick.

So I begin get up small, small, begin dey move, dey push bush and leaves and trees one side. By this time, I just forget all those bad anmals that are inside the forest. I only remember Dukana, my mama and Agnes and how I must see them quick quick. So I was moving inside that forest. As I am moving now, I come see say the trees no too plenty again. I come see after some time say the sun dey shine plenty and I know that I must not move for day time. So when I reach the place wey tree no dey again and na soso bush, I come stop. Then I just lie down and sleep.

I think I sleep for long time, because when I come open my eye, the sun have dead. Only one big moon like football was shining. Hungry catch me well well and I tire proper proper. But I know that I cannot waste time whether I hungry or I no hungry. I just beg God make 'e help me make my body strong, make I fit walk plenty that night. I beg God make 'e show me the way I go take reach my mama house. So I look as the moon was standing and I come remember that for Dukana, the moon used to rise from our backyard. So I just follow the moon. I no fit walk fast, but I walk plenty. And I must to be careful because as you know, anything can happen during war. It is possible for the enemy to move for night. And if they catch me, only God know whether I will see my mama again. But even though I walk plenty, because I am walking careful, I know that I cannot go very far. And the bush no be any man friend. So I was walking that whole night. And as you know, I was still not very well. And after some time, day begin break small small. And as I was very tired, I just fall down for one place sleep.

When I woke up, the sun was not shining at all. Every place dark well well. I begin to think that some time night have come. But it is lie. It was big big cloud in the sky. I know that it is going to rain and my heart begin cut because I am hungry and I am sure that this rain will give me plenty *wahala* because of no place to hide. No tree anywhere at all. Only bush and farm. Bush and farm. And true true before you can count two, it was raining plenty plenty. I am telling you I have not seen such rain before since long time and I was not happy as the rain come beat me for body and begin make small river for ground. Everywhere na soso water. So I just ask myself who born dog? Who born dog?

It rained the whole of the time. I does not know whether it is night or day. Moon did not come out. Sun did not shine. And I cannot move even one step at all. And no cloth for my body only short knicker and plenty wound for my leg and my hand and all my bone just tire like dog who have run plenty. And still that rain does not stop. After some time it will come be like say it wants to stop. And it will fall small small, small small. Then it will come heavy again. Just like that. Plenty, plenty, small small. And all that time, I was inside the rain. Sometime I will stand and after I have tired for stand, then I will try to sit. But all the time, there is nowhere to sit at all at all. I begin to beg God make the rain stop. But impossible. That rain continue to beat me and after it have beat me well well, I come consider myself like anmal. Yes, I was like anmal. No shirt, only knicker, wound for my body, no food to chop, no house to sleep, only inside bush and rain beating me like no man business. Oh my God, why has thou forsaken me? That is what I was saying to myself as they used to say in the Bible. Oh my God, why has thou forsaken me? Have I tiefed? Have I called another man's wife? I am good young man. I obey my mama every time. And I have married a fine young woman. And even in the war I am behaving like gentleman. I don't like to kill anybody or anything. I have not even shoot gun one day or even one time. At all at all. And I am just doing what they tell me to do. So why oh God, I am suffering like this? I tell my God that I do not like this war and if he can stop the rain and help me to go back to Dukana, I will never wear any uniform or carry gun again. I beg God to forgive me if I have done some bad thing before. That I will never do such bad thing again. And then I come die again.

LOMBER SIXTEEN

When I opened my eyes, I was in one long dormitory where everybody get bandage for leg or for him body. At first I think this is land of spirit. I begin to shout and hala like idiot man. Then one man came and chooked me and I come sleep one time like stupid goat. I think the man who chooked me this chooking is Manmuswak. That is what I was thinking as I was going to sleep after he have chooked me. Always I see that face of very tall man and I think it is somebody that I have seen before. But sleep is catching me quick quick and I cannot see the face again.

I cannot tell you how long I sleep. But I think I sleep for very long time. Because when I wake up, I will not see anything and then I will know it is night time. And then I will see Manmuswak face as it was that time in Iwoama when he was giving us hot drink and cigar. And then I will see his face again as he was chooking me the chook. And then everything will confuse and I will sleep again. And then I will wake up afterwards. Always like that. All the time. Until I come open my eye well well and I cannot sleep again.

So I rub my eye and I am alive and awake. I look round the hospital dormitory and I see that very tall man again. Yes, my dear brothers and sisters, it is Manmuswak. Manmuswak is here again. Oh, I cannot tell you how my heart just cut when I see this Manmuswak in the hospital. He is now nurse and chooking people with needle. What does all this mean? Am I prisoner of war? What happened to me in that bush? And why must I always see this Manmuswak man? First it is in African Upwine Bar in New York, Diobu, then in the war front at Iwoama and now in the hospital dormitory. So he is good-time-man drinking *tombo* and dancing; then he is soza making cunny to scatter one camp and kill everybody; and now he is nurse, smiling and chooking porson.

And when I tell you that he is smiling, I am not joking you know. He is actually smiling. And talking to me like better man, this tall man, Manmuswak. He is telling me that 'e remain small I for die. He is telling me that I have been sleeping in that bed for more than one week. One week! To God who made me! He said that all that one week, I am just shouting and talking every time about Dukana and my mama and Agnes with J.J.C. And he have been chooking me and giving me medicine and some chop and drink. So when I see that he is like my friend and brother, I begin to ask him how I got to that hospital.

"Well, we found you in the bush. You have almost dead because of hunger and tiredness, and your body have blow up like big dead fish floating on water and you cannot talk." That is what Manmuswak said, as I hear 'am.

"True?" I asked.

"Oh yes. You were talking mambo-jambo like stupid idiot goat." Mambo-jambo. I like that word. Mambo-jambo. And that is what I was talking when I came to the hospital the first time.

"Terrible," I said.

"And after that you begin hala about your Mama and one Agnes with J.J.C."

"Is that so?"

"Yes," Manmuswak replied. "So we have to chook you so you can sleep and forget about your Agnes."

"Thank you very much, sah," I said.

When I wanted to ask him about the porson who get the hospital and whether I am prisoner of war or what, he just put him hand for him mouth. Which mean that I must not ask him such question at all.

I do not know who I can ask the question that is worrying my mind very much. Because all the people who are lying in that hospital are very very sick. Some of them are shouting and crying. Others are talking mambo-jambo. Mambo-jambo. And some are ready to die. Those who die, they just carry them throway like dead cockroach. And the whole hospital is smelling one kain, one kain. And you know, it is not proper hospital oh. It is actually school with blackboard on the wall everywhere. Only because of the war they have turned it to hospital dormitory.

And as I do not know anybody in that place, I said to myself that after all said and done, they are all enemy sozas. But if they are enemy sozas, why did they not kill me that time when they see me for inside bush? If they kill me, will anybody know? How about all those that they are killing everytime with bomb and gun? Why should they sorry for me and not sorry for those people? Or praps they want to do me some very bad thing after I have get well, so they do not want to kill me now now. Or praps they do not like to kill soza who is not well. Or soza who is not fat like llama. And as I am not well and I am not fat, they will not like to kill me yet.

After some time, I begin to get well. And I am moving small small in that hospital school looking at the other sick sozas. And talking to the sozas who are the nurse. Every time, I will try to make them laugh so that they will all like me. Even Manmuswak used to come to me to knack tory after he have chooked the sick sozas. So he told me how he have fought the war in many places. I asked him whether all the place he have fight for na soso nurse wey 'e be. Manmuswak laugh one kain laugh. With plenty tooth for him mouth. He told me that his work is war. And war mean many things to soza like himself. You can be anything when there is war. He say that he can carry gun and dead body. Chooking needle and grenade. And he is really soza. He will fight if they just tell him to fight. Anywhere. Anytime. And he must obey because orders is orders. And no nonsense. He can fight and kill his brother, he does not care. He can be friend today and enemy tomorrow. He does not care. Once it is war.

As he was speaking, I can see that this Manmuswak is very wicked man. This is because of how his face was very strong and tight. And his eyes very red. I remembered how he was talking that day at African Upwine Bar, and how he have used cunny to break our Company. And even though he have picked me up from the bush and he is chooking me morning and night till I am well, and he is talking to me as my friend, I believe that he is just making cunny and he can kill me anytime. Because as him work be war, he cannot mind what he does to any porson who is soza or even not soza but porson staying where they are fighting.

To talk true, from that day I begin to see this Manmuswak every time that I am sleeping. Or even when I am awake. He will come to me and he will say "You idiot Sozaboy, you think I do not know how you and Bullet have killed your soza captain and how you have run away in the bush killing small small anmals and chopping them. You don't know that any soza who run away from fighting is runaway soza and if they catch him he must be shoot like llama. All this one that I am giving you food and chooking you medicine you don't know I am just making you to fat like llama so that we can shoot you and you can go and join your friend Bullet. Sozaboy, just wait for me. I will show you pepper. One day be one day. I am Manmuswak and you must fear me. As everybody who have hear my name in war front must fear me. Because I am soza and I am war. I have no friend and I can fight anybody whether whether." So I begin fear either for sleep oh or for morning or afternoon or evening. The fear no gree make I chop. I did not want to fat like llama. Some time if I am not fat, Manmuswak and his people will not think of killing me.

One day, Manmuswak came to me in the morning after he have treated and chooked all de sick sozas. He said to me that he have seen that I have refused to eat food since long time. That do I know what I am doing? That I am trying to make hunger strike. To show that I am stronghead soza. That I am trying to escape. So I told Manmuswak that it is not so. So he asked me why I am refusing to eat. And when I cannot tell him why because to talk true by this time I was fearing him to nonsense, he told me that as I am stronghead soza, he will tell his soza captain that I am well now and that I must go to the front of the war again. When Manmuswak talk about the war front, I begin to cry. Because by this time, I do not like war at all. All that talk that Zaza was talking about Burma, I just no like at all. All the things that I have seen at Pitakwa and Iwoama I just did not want to see again. All I am thinking is how I will go to Dukana to see my mama and my Agnes J.J.C. So I began to think how I will just run away from that school hospital. But when I look outside I see many many sozas. I am sure all these sozas are enemy and they are all waiting to kill me. Then I have to wait and plan again how to run away.

Then another day, Manmuswak told me that the soza captain wants to see me. I just get up follow Manmuswak like goat that they are to kill. My heart was beating drum, *bam – bam – bam –' bam – bam – bam – bam*. So, true true, they want to kill me. I wanted to cry, I cannot. I wanted to talk to Manmuswak, fear did not allow me. I just followed Manmuswak like goat sotey we reach the soza captain office. By this time, I am like dead goat only I never begin smell, and blood did not come out of my body.

So as soon I got to the soza captain office, he just shouted "Attention!" As they have teach us before for camp in Pitakwa, I just stand straight with my hands down like stick. So the soza captain say "Yes, you are a soza all right."

"I am not a soza," is what I replied.

"You are telling lies," is what the soza captain said.

"No sah."

"You are not? Then what are you?"

"I am apprentice driver."

"Apprentice driver? Can you drive a car? Do you have a licence?" I told him that I can drive. That I have licence but the licence have lost when the sozas were fighting in my village.

"Good, good, good," the soza captain replied. "You know how to drive and you know how to shoot."

"No sah, I don't know how to shoot," is what I replied.

"Okay, we'll teach you how to shoot," was his reply.

Oh God in Heaven, why have you decide to punish me like this? What have I done? Have I called another man's wife? Have I disobeyed anybody at all? Is it because my mama said I should not go to the sozas and I did not agree that you want to show me pepper like this? Oh God, I beg you by name of Agnes my young wife with J.J.C. let them not kill me today. I take God beg una make una no kill me today.

This is what I was saying to myself. My teeth were shaking

like truck on the road and my feet were dancing on the ground. I am telling you, fear catch *helele*. So the soza captain began to laugh small small, small small. I think when he saw how I was shaking like idiot *mumu*, he was sorry for me. He said that he will not worry me, because he have seen that I can be useful man specially as I have driving licence and I can shoot. I began to cry. I told the soza captain that I cannot shoot, that I am not soza at all since I was born.

No sooner I have said this than I hear a voice behind me shouting *Quashun! Staat eese! Ajuwaya!* I immediately stand attention and stand at ease too like good soza. So the soza captain begin laugh. He laughed for long time. Then he asked Manmuswak where he get idiot man like myself from. Manmuswak say he picked me like snail from the bush. He said I have already dead sef by the time he saw me and if he had not put me in hospital and give me plenty medicine and food I will have dead long ago. The soza captain said if so, they should just finish the work that God have begin. I knew at once that the soza captain is telling them to kill me. And I just fall down and cry. I was begging the soza captain not to kill me. Please. Because true true I am good man. I will do anything they ask me to do. I will even carry shit. I will be his houseboy and slave, anything, but I do not want to die. Because I am young. I do not mind to go to the war front sef. I will tell him everything that our big man told us that day when we finish our training before we go to the front. I beg the big man. I beg Manmuswak. I beg Manmuswak to beg the big man so that they will not kill me that day. And God heard my prayer. Because after some time, as I was still lying on the ground crying and holding the big man leg, he commanded me to get up. So I got up quick. He said that he will not waste any ammo on useless man like myself. He told Manmuswak to go give me twenty-four and after that babar me properly and put me in Kampala. That he will think what he will do with me after. Praps he will cut my tongue so that I will not tell lie again. That is what he said.

Immediately, Manmuswak took me away and he marched me to one part of the field. Left, right, left, right, left, right, left! Only God can tell what Manmuswak did to me that day. By the time he finished flogging me with horsewhip or *koboko*, my body was covered with blood. I begin to pray to die. I think it is better to die than to stay alive and suffer as I was suffering that day. Then they shaved all my hair and then they locked me inside one small hut. There were many of us inside there. All the time we were inside, they did not bring us any food. Only small water. And you cannot even go out to piss or shit. We all piss and shit in that small useless prison. I begin ask myself why I disobeyed my mama and went to join the army.

I stayed in that guardroom for one week. I was counting every day and every night. And every time I will remember that this is not the end of my punishment. Because the soza captain have said that he will cut my tongue so that I will not tell lie again. And any time they are bringing us water to drink, I will begin to fear that maybe the time that they will cut my tongue have reached. As fear did not kill me that week, I know that fear cannot kill me again for the rest of my life. I am telling you the fear of punishment *worwor* pass the punishment. I used to stay there and see as Manmuswak will come to me with long sharp knife in one hand and then he will hold my tongue with the other hand. He will ask me to push my tongue forward and then use two fingers to hold the bottom of my tongue. And I will be shouting or trying to shout. Then he will actually carry his hand up and then – cut my tongue from far inside my mouth. And then I will swallow the blood. And sometime he will give me my tongue to chop or praps he will bury it or praps take it away and show it to the big man before he will take it to his home to cook and eat. And after I have seen this thing for my mind eye, I will use my finger to touch my tongue so that I can know if it is still there. It was there. Every time when I wake up in the morning, I will touch it and before I sleep in the night, I will also touch it. Wonders will never end. My tongue was still there. And seven days have passed since the soza big man promised to cut it. Or sometimes the man have forgotten what he promised to do. God, please help him to forget well well.

Then one morning, I heard Manmuswak calling me. "Sozaboy! Sozaboy!" I jumped up one time. I said to myself, Sozaboy your life don spoil today. "Sozaboy!" "Sozaboy!" Manmuswak continued to shout like mad man. Fear catch me *helele*. Then he came inside and hold my neck and push me out of that prison hut. I wanted to run but fear does not allow me. I just fall down for ground like pillow. Manmuswak laugh. He laughed plenty. Then he came and hold my right hand and began to tell me that if I am not driver and I have talked that I am driver, true true I will see pepper because as the soza boss have forgive me for the first time that I told lie, this time if I tell lie again it is not only my tongue they will cut, they will cut my *prick* and my *blokkus* too and they will cook all of them for me to eat without my tongue. So I told him that, true true, I am a proper driver and I can drive any car or motor or caterpillar. So Manmuswak say okay, if everything is as I talk, then I am very lucky man. But if it is lie, make I go back inside the belly of the mama who born me. Because by the time he have finish with me I will regret that they born me at all. So he gave me one key and he asked me to run inside the Land Rover that was in front of the dormitory hospital.

I tell you I was very happy. I just no waste time at all. I took the key and ran inside the motor one time. I think you know that to talk true I am not actually driver. I have not get licence and although I can fit to move the motor small, I never drive long way before but I know that if I enter the motor, I can move it. And as motors are not plenty on the road, I think I will be able to reach anywhere I am going.

Nevertheless I entered that land rover and I moved it as I am praying to God plenty so that I will not mess up my senior commando and Manmuswak begin take me make *ye-ye*. And you know, as something used to happen, I actually moved that land rover. I moved it. No trouble at all. I drove. I drove. I drove. No accident. I turned it in the compound. I entered the main road. I revised. I went front, anything I like, I just did. And I was prouding of myself because, before before, my master will not even allow me to hold the steering wheel. Only when he is not there that I will hide and hold the steering and begin move the motor small small. But today, I know that water will pass *gari* if I just formfool. And God come help me, *sha*.

So when I returned the landrover, I saw that Manmuswak was just smiling and laughing, smiling and laughing. And when I quenched the engine and jumped down, he just beat me on the back and shouted "Sozaboy, you getu luck-uo! Sozaboy, you getu luck-uo! So na from prisoner of war to driver ehn? And I no go get chance to chop dat your big big prick! God don butter your bread, Sozaboy."

I was prouding of myself, I am telling you. Everything was very very nice for me now. I know at once that they will not kill me like llama. That by God's power I will reach Dukana and I will see my mama and my young wife Agnes with J.J.C. Oh God, help me please, I beg you. Don't allow me to suffer again because I have suffer too much already.

And true true, God hear my prayer well well. From that day, everything begin good for me. Because they gave me uniform again. Immediately I wear that uniform I know that I am not prisoner of war. That they will not shoot me like llama. And it is not just uniform oh. They also gave me one short thick rifle like this. Very fine rifle. I like it. I held it in my hand as I for hold Agnes my young wife with J.J.C. I told the rifle that him and me we will sleep and wake together and if anybody come disturb us, we will just finish him one time. Ah-ah. And na these people they are calling 'enemy' all the time. How enemy will give me chop, chook me medicine till I well, give me motor to drive without I no get licence, give me fine fine uniform and then very fantastic rifle. So I am a fool all this time that I am wanting to kill this enemy! God of mercy!

Then I begin to think how with the landrover that they will give me to drive I will reach Dukana one day. And when they will see me in my uniform and driving army land rover, I am sure that they will be prouding of me because true true I am not just Sozaboy for mouth, but Sozaboy proper proper and even more than that Zaza with loin cloth shouting every time about Burma and no Burma and Hitla and no Hitla although he have no money and no work and even sef no cloth. In fact if Zaza see me now he cannot talk and even if he talk, I think I will just show him. Just beat him small, slap him small, throw him inside the land rover and make him prisoner of peace to show him that the fight of nowadays is different from the fight of olden days. Then I come think how the people of Dukana will think if they see me in enemy uniform. I just cancel that from my mind because I don't want to think such useless thing today that I am in new uniform with rifle and driving land rover without driving licence.

I will not tell you all the things that happen during the time that I was driving that land rover because it is very very long tory. Nevertheless I can tell you that Manmuswak and myself become very good friend because every time, Manmuswak will be sending me message. Or he will go out with me. All the time it is not our proper soza work that Manmuswak is doing. Sometimes he will go to people farm and tief their yams and plantain and go and sell it. Sometime he will go another man house who have run beause of fear of gun and bomb and he will take away the bed and the iron pot and anything that is fine for eye and which he think he can sell. Then he will go and sell it and put the money in his pocket. Always I will be watching him or he will give me order to help him work him work. And I must obey him as soza concern. So everyday I was working and driving but I can never take money from Manmuswak because my mama have told me never to tief anything because everyday is for the tief but one day is for the owner of the house. So I myself do not like to tief and all the time all I am thinking is how I will just go back to Dukana and see my people. I promise myself that one day I will go to them in the land rover.

And as God does something, after two months Manmuswak begin to send me message all by myself. All this time that I am talking, the war is still going on oh. I used to carry message to war front every time with Manmuswak. And I will be seeing how there is nobody for road at all only sometimes rotten man or woman with soso bone and sometimes a dog looking for something to chop. True true, every time when I see something like that, I will just remember Bullet and all those boys in my group who are now spirits all because of this Manmuswak who have saved my own life. And then I will remember that war is useless nonsense and all this uniform and everything is just to cause confusion and make porson fine like goat that they have make fat and ready to kill for chop during Christmas. So I was not very happy.

LOMBER SEVENTEEN

Many of the villages that I always see when I am driving to the front or returning to our camp in the hospital school are all empty. No porson living there, or if porson is living there, then that porson is hiding. And all the houses have fall down or just ready to fall down because the bullet have made hole in the roof and the rain have entered the house and there is nobody to take care of anything at all. And all the time I am thinking that that is how Dukana must be. And still I am praying that God must help my mama and my young wife Agnes with J.J.C.

By this time, the soza boss and Manmuswak like me like their brother. Because any message that they send me I must go well well and no mistake. Even money does not loss for my hand. And I begin to learn more about the engine of the motor so that my motor was not spoiling plenty as other driver motor used to spoil. But I did not tell Manmuswak anything about my mama and my young wife Agnes with J.J.C. I did not tell him about Dukana and how I must go there one day. Because whether Manmuswak is my brother today, he can just change his mind any time if he see that I am formfooling. I think you understand me. Because war is war and I am sure that this Manmuswak and the soza boss and all the sozas sef are just like my rifle. If you send them message, they must go, and the message to all the sozas in this war as I understand it is, as the soza boss tell me one day, 'To kill or to be killed'. To kill or to be killed. I will not forget that one at all. And I am sure that Manmuswak have put it for his mind whether he is asleep or he is eating.

But as I was saying I know that one day will be one day. One day must be one day. So one day when they send me message to war front, I go the message quick. As I war returning, I don't know the thing that enter my head. I just drive my motor to Dukana side. I just forget Manmuswak and the soza boss and the message that they have sent me. I was thinking of Dukana and my mama and my young wife Agnes with J.J.C. I just put speed and go. Something happen to me that day. I just no mind whether they will beat me when I return to the hospital school camp. Or whether they will put me for Kampala or whether they will shoot me. I just want to see my people. Full stop. So I drove on that very bad road till I reached Dukana.

Oh, God of mercy. When I see my home town Dukana, I could not talk. You know, all that time that I am driving and seeing those empty towns, 'e no too pain me. But when I see my own home town, I begin cry. I reach there for afternoon time. I did not see anybody *lai lai*. I drove the motor with plenty noise. I blow the horn. Nobody. I go everywhere. Nobody. All the houses were just there. Some of the doors are closed, others the doors are open. But nobody at all. Even one porson. And no goat or chicken or anything at all. Everywhere just silent like church on Monday. No noise. Even no bird is singing or talking in Dukana. Impossible. Only plenty grass everywhere. Everywhere. Even some of the road have begin to close because of grass. Soso grass. Even in the pot that is outside the house. I go for my mama house. I open the door and enter. Very bad smell enter my nose because, as you know, mud must smell very bad if it is raining and no fire in the house. I looked everywhere inside the house. I see that my mama and my young wife Agnes with J.J.C. have took time to remove all their things. Which mean that they did not run away quickly. Even all my own cloth, they have taken away too. Ah – ah. Or did somebody come to tief all our things? The only thing I see in the house is just empty pot and mortar and bucket. Nothing again. Not even cockroach or rat. So I go to Agnes him mama house. The same thing. No cloth, no anything, only pot and mortar and bucket and no cockroach or rat.

Then one mind come tell me that I must go either the farm or fishing port or where they used to tap palm wine. So as all these places are in one place, I went there. I was walking, holding the rifle with one hand. And the other hand will be clearing the bush and grass from the road so I can pass. Na so I was going until I see some smoke smoking small small from behind some trees. I followed the smoke until I reach the hut from where it was coming from. Then I entered the hut. Nobody there. Ah – ah? I looked round carefully. There was one calabash of palm wine on the floor. And another pot of palmy was on the fire which is where the smoke was coming from. That is what old men in Dukana used to do during the rainy season; they have to warm their palmy before they drink it. So therefore, it means that there is old man in that hut or near the hut, in the bush, hiding.

So I went out and made noise with my mouth. No answer. Then I returned to the hut and begin to look carefully. I see one big dirty cloth like tarpaulin on the floor. So I used the rifle on the tarpaulin. Then I hear one big shout: "I beg-oh, I beg-oh." I cannot make mistake for the voice. It is Duzia.

"Duzia," I called.

"My lord," he answered from under the tarpaulin.

So I pulled the tarpaulin away. And what I saw are two men hiding under the cloth. Duzia and Bom were hiding.

"Duzia, Bom," I shouted, "So you are here. Thank God." Duzia and Bom did not answer me one word. I can see that they are very afraid. Shaking like leaf. Even I don't think that they know me.

"Duzia, I am Sozaboy," I said.

Duzia just look on the ground. Bom did not even open his eyes. After some time, Duzia said, "If you want kill me, do it quick quick, no wasting time."

"I don't want to kill you," I replied.

"Then what do you want?" he asked.

"I am your own Sozaboy, from this very town, Dukana. Look at me."

"Sozaboy have already dead," Duzia said.

"No. I am not dead. Look at me. I am the same Sozaboy. Look at me."

Duzia did not even bother to look. He shook his head plenty.

"Sozaboy have already dead," he said.

"Duzia, look at me. I am not dead. I am Sozaboy. Your Sozaboy. Touch me."

So now, Duzia looked at me. Then he shook his head. "This is not the uniform of our own Sozaboy. You are putting the uniform of enemy sozas. You are not our own Sozaboy," he said. All this time, Bom did not say one word. He was still shaking with fear. So I come see that I must do something to convince these people that I am their son and friend and townsman. So I pour some of the palm wine from the calabash and I sit down to drink. No sooner the drink enter my belly than I hear my name "Sozaboy." It is Duzia.

"Yes," I answered.

"Bom, Bom," Duzia called, "you two-legged quack, here is smallpox Sozaboy himself; he have come back from the land of ghost."

"I don't believe it," Bom said. "It cannot be Sozaboy. Sozaboy have already dead in the army. If he is here, it must be his ghost."

"I am not ghost," I said, "Look at me. I am Sozaboy."

"And what are you looking for here?" Bom asked.

"I have come to see what is happening in Dukana. To look for you and my mama and my wife Agnes and all the other people."

"You travelled all the way from grave to come and look for us."

"I have never dead," is what I answered.

"You have already dead long ago. Look now, the soza uniform you are wearing is different. You are not our own Sozaboy. You are ghost," Bom said.

Look ehn, as Bom was saying this thing was a great surprisation to me. I did not think that he is serious. But Duzia is saying the same thing too. What do they mean?

"What do you mean?" I asked.

"Because you died at Iwoama long time ago. During the big fighting when the enemy have blow up your Company and camp and everybody was killed. You died that time," Duzia said.

"I did not die. Is a lie. I did not die."

"What happened?"

"Duzia, my brother, is a long tory, true true. But the fact is, I do not die that time. I no get even wound sef."

"True?"

"To God who born me. Is true that many sozas die that day. But me, I no get even wound."

"Sozaboy. Juju. Smallpox. Dukana Boy!" Duzia said prouding. "And everybody was saying that you have already dead. Because we do not hear about you for long time. And you do not come home and you do not write letter as sozas used to do."

"I was very sick after that fight at Iwoama. I sleep in forest for long time after all my friends have already dead."

"No wonder. Eh, Bom, you two-legged quack, do you hear the wonderful tory that I am hearing from this our wonder boy?"

"I am listening," Bom replied.

"Wonders will never end. And already everybody was crying for you. Everybody in Dukana."

"Is that so?"

Duzia and Bom drank some palmy and then they spit on the ground. Then they look at me for long time. Then they speak to each other in small voice. Then Duzia said, as I hear 'am: "Sozaboy, juju, I will talk to you. If you are ghost, or you are living porson as you talk, I will still talk to you because what my eye have seen, my mouth cannot talk it."

"Please talk to me," I said, as I sat down on the floor of the hut.

"Since you left Dukana, Sozaboy, nothing have gone well for our people. That is why I call you smallpox. No. You are juju sef. You are the only Dukana boy who gree to goin the sozas. And since you left us nothing go well for all of us. I was praying that you should come back to show all these useless sozas pepper. To free us from the hand of the sozas. They used to enter the houses in the night and fuck the women by force, drink the pot of soup and take away the yams. They ask us to go to the swamp and cut the mangrove because the enemy sozas are hiding there. Oh Sozaboy, juju, smallpox, your brothers, your fathers, your mother and your wife suffered more than I can tell you. Every night, we have to return to our house very early and shut the door. Then sometimes we will hear the aeroplane flying in the sky. It was very frightening. I used to hear how the bombs will drop from the sky and kill person. I did not know that I will see it in my lifetime. When the time came, I did not know. We were all sitting in the playground talking and thinking what we will do when the sozas come again to byforce our women and drink the pot of soup and take away the yams and beat the men. Suddenly, we heard the sound of aeroplane in the sky. It flew many times round Dukana. Going round and round all the time. By this time we are all like banana leaf. The women were shouting. The men were running from one place to another place telling the women and children to enter house. Then the aeroplane came down like hawk wanting to catch hen. Wham, bang! bang! bang! When we opened our eyes, the church, the old church was broken with big hole in roof. Pastor Barika was crying like small picken. Sozaboy, juju, smallpox, what happened that day was a terrible thing. But it was small to compare what happened the day after that and the day after that and the day after that and the day after that. God forbid. Every afternoon the plane will come. We were like rabbit. We did not know what to do. But even the plane was a good thing because it will come and go. Sometimes all the bomb dropping from the plane used to fall in the farm and nobody was killed.

Then one day, we begin to hear the noise of gun. It is like one thousand double-barrel shooting at the same time. It can block porson ear. And it used to cut our heart. When the gun begin shooting, it was very far away. Then it begin to come nearer and nearer. Sozaboy, smallpox, I am telling you, since my mother born me, I have never been frightened like that. Chief Birabee was crying before everybody.

"Then the sozas who have been beating us and chopping our food every day come back to Dukana. This time they came with their heavy guns. And they drove us from our house. There was no place for us to sleep again. Then they began to shoot their own gun. The noise and trouble in Dukana was too much. All those who have two legs begin to run away. Sozaboy, juju, I looked at myself, I cannot run. And there is no place for me to run to. Because I have no father and mother anywhere in this world. And where can somebody run that the shooting will not reach or the bomb will not reach? And it was raining from morning till night. To talk true some of those people who ran away were running because of fear. And if you do not have strong heart, you cannot hear all these guns and still stay in the same place.

"Soon only few of us remained for Dukana. We cannot go to the farm. We cannot go and draw water from the stream. There was nothing to eat and drink. Life was very hard. Even Zaza who is old soza was crying like small picken because his people have all run away. One day, the sozas begin to put all their guns in lorry. Then they asked all remaining people in Dukana to enter the lorry. By this time Bom and myself were already hiding in the bush. Bom used to go near Dukana to see what is happening. He is the one who used to come back to tell me everything. The stupid sozas took away their guns and our people in the morning. In the evening, the other sozas, the enemy arrived. Bom saw them running about in Dukana doing the same thing that the other sozas used to do. Cutting the plantains and bananas and digging yams. Killing the goats and hen. Sozaboy, juju, all you sozas are the same thing. I don't like to see any soza in my life again.

"By this time I am telling you, the plane is not passing over Dukana again. The guns are not sounding again. I know that if there is any more fight, the fight will not happen here. What it means is that our people have run to where they are going to begin to fight again. When I think of all this, I know that Dukana people will suffer for long long time. So Bom and myself begin to make this hut here. Then we begin to look for food and palm wine. And that is how we have been living every day for more than six month. Everyday, Bom will go to Dukana to see whether anybody have returned from the war. Every day he will see that nobody have returned. Tomorrow he will go again to see whether the people have returned. And he will return again because no one have returned. I used to ask myself where all the people have gone. But I cannot find any answer. After some time, Sozaboy, juju, I begin to thank God that I have no leg to run with. Because if I have leg, I am sure I will not be here today, drinking palmy and eating roast yam. Sozaboy, juju, smallpox, I am telling you, I am living like a king these days. All the yam and plantain that our people planted, no one to eat them. Aa! ha! only myself and this foolish man, Bom. But I tell you, it is not something that porson can be proud about. Because Dukana is not like Dukana again. Where are Chief Birabee them and all those his chiefs who every time will take bribe from the people? Where is Pastor Barika singing his song in the morning and in the evening and every Sunday telling all his lies from the pulpit to the women of Dukana? Where are all the young men with their long *prick* and big *blokkus*? And where are all the young young girls with J.J.C. just waiting for the young men? Sozaboy, smallpox, juju, Dukana don die. The war have buried our town."

I listened to Duzia very well, and I tell you, I was almost crying; only as sozaman concern, I must preserve my persy at all times. And you know, this Duzia is very queer man. Because he know well well the thing I am very much wanted to hear. He will not tell me that thing. He just wants me to continue to suffer so that he can laugh at me. So after I have listened to his long long tory, I come ask Duzia about my mama and my young wife Agnes. So he spoke in small voice to Bom for some time. Then he told me.

"Ah, your young wife Agnes with J.J.C. and your mama. You know, after the fighting at Iwoama everybody was saying that you have already dead. Your mama and your wife cried plenty. As you are your mama's only son, the thing pain am pass. She was saying how she did not want you to join soza. And you took stronghead and run away and now you are dead. Everybody was very sorry for her. In fact, I used to see her plenty. She was crying from morning to night. She refused to eat; she does not go to farm again. Only your wife was taking care of her. All the time she will sit with her and beg her not to cry again because she thinks that her husband, her Sozaboy is brave man and cannot die. I am sure that if not for Agnes, your mama will have already dead because of unhappiness."

I was very happy to hear that. Oh, thank God.

"But true true, your young wife Agnes with J.J.C. is another sozaman wife now. You know as you sozas are. You all like woman. And you like beautiful woman more than. When I see how that you Agnes is walking all the time, I know that one soza man or even soza captain will just take her and make her his war wife. And that is what happened, Sozaboy, juju. But make you no worry. You will find another wife any time anywhere in this world. If you are still alive and not ghost. After all, as fish borku for river na so woman borku for the world. So if you lose one woman you must not cry because you will get another one, and even better one sef." That is what Duzia replied.

Bom drank the palmy, belched and spit on the ground. Then he blow his nose and rubbed his palms together. "Soza and woman. They all too like woman," Bom said.

I was very angry with this stupid man but I cannot say anything to him because I did not want to quarrel with him and I just want them to tell me what have happened to my dear mama afterwards when the bomb and gun begin to reach Dukana and as they said everybody come take fear run commot. But no need for me to ask sef because after some time, after those two men have drunk some more palmy, Duzia told me that he think my mama was taken away by the sozaman who took my wife Agnes. He said that my mama was crying all the time and Agnes was crying too so therefore the sozaman took two of them away.

Then Bom said it is not so. That although the sozaman like my wife Agnes, he have no motor to use to carry them so he asked them to trek and run away from Dukana because of the bomb and the guns. And he himself have seen my mama running away with Agnes. They have no clothes and no food and he does not know where they are running to because after some time, he saw that sozaman again in their house and he thinks that the enemy sozas have killed him.

All these different stories were making me very very unhappy. I do not know which one to believe. But what I know is that my mama and Agnes with J.J.C. are not in Dukana. And they have not dead. I know that I must look for them immediately.

I did not want to stay with Duzia and Bom again so I come give them the money that I have in my pocket. Duzia just laugh. 'E tell me thank you but I should put my money in my pocket because himself and Bom do not want money. They have the yams and the cassava and plantain and banana of the whole of

Dukana and even if they live for one hundred years, they cannot finish the food. And what will they use the money for in the bush? Bom told me to keep the money and go and use it to look for Chief Birabee and my mama and my wife if they have not already dead. And he said I must to be careful because everybody is enemy in this our war. There is nobody to trust. Your friend today can be your enemy tomorrow. He said that devil and juju have entered the mind and eye of everybody and only God can save somebody.

So after they have told me all these things, I just went straight to my land rover and drove away. I did not look back. I did not look right. I did not look left. Tears just plenty for my eye but I cannot cry. As I was driving I was thinking to myself how I will just drive the land rover straight to the war front and I will just cross to the other side to see if my people are there. Then I said to myself that that will be stealing and I remember as my mama used to talk that everyday is for tiefman but one day is for the owner. And then since Manmuswak have saved my life before and given me land rover to drive too, I think that it will not be good to run away and also to tief land rover. God will not forgive me if I come do that kain thing. So, I say okay, I will return the motor but I must go away because I cannot stay with that Manmuswak and enemy soza and say that I am helping them to fight the fight when I do not know where my people are. So I just drove the motor reach the camp. By this time night have come. I just *dabara* the motor there, leave the key inside and take my rifle and go.

LOMBER EIGHTEEN

I walked all that night. I did not even know where I was going. I have no food. And no water. And no money. To talk true, I was not thinking of all these things, I was just thinking of my mama and my young wife Agnes. If my mama die, what will I talk? If that sozaman have pregnanted my young darling or even sef killed her because she no gree 'am, what will I say? Ah, God no gree bad thing, God no gree bad thing. I must to find my mama and my wife. We must to all return to Dukana and build fine house to live inside. As I am now qualified driver, I will just get licence and I will find lorry to drive. Then I will get plenty money and my mama and Agnes and myself will be happy. And some time I fit buy my own lorry afterwards; then from the profit I will buy another lorry and another one and then another one again. And I will employ driver to drive the lorries but I will not allow them to tief my money as my master used to tief his master money. This is what I was thinking as I was walking along the road.

After some time, I begin think how Manmuswak dem fit follow me for back if they look for me and they cannot see me. So I know that I will not stay in the main road whether it is night or in the day. I just enter one time for bush as soon as I see one small road. I just follow that road. I follow am sotey I tire. I just lie down for ground come sleep.

When I open my eye, day have broke well well. I come remember everything that happened yesterday and I say to myself that I must go ahead and take my mama and my Agnes from the war. I hold my rifle for hand and I swear to myself that if anybody stop me or try to stop me from what I am trying to do, I must kill that porson first. And even if that man is that useless Chief Commander General, nobody can stop me from killing him. Although I have not eaten since yesterday, I am not hungry at all. I do not know exactly where I am going, but I think that if I just move with the sun on my right in the morning or on my left in the evening, everything will be awright. And I know that I must stay in the bush all the time. God so kind all that time that I was working with Manmuswak, they used to send me to the front and so I have known where all the sozas are staying in their pits and where they are shooting their guns. And I know that I must not go near these sozas because anything can happen as war is war. So I began to walk along the bush road. I walked very quick and I was not tired even though I have not eaten and I have not drink any water.

But as I was going, I begin to ask myself why I am going inside the bush instead of going to Pitakwa first of all. If Agnes is running from Dukana is it not Pitakwa that she will go to before any place? Because is it not only Pitakwa and Lagos that she knows? And I know that the sozas have finished fighting in Pitakwa proper. They are fighting in all those small small villages near Pitakwa but they are not fighting inside Pitakwa now. As you know, I call all of them sozas now because I have seen that they are all two and two pence. I will not allow anybody to tell me that this is enemy and the other one is not enemy. They are all doing the same thing and as Manmuswak and Tan Papa used to say, "war is war." So in fact I begin to go to Pitakwa.

I am not walking along the road but inside the bush near the road. And to talk true I was fearing *helele*. Because inside that bush are many dead bodies. And all these dead bodies are just smelling one kain one kain. Very very poongent. And when I see them, I used to ask myself every time, is this the picken that when him mama born am everybody was very happy and dancing and drinking because he have bring human being into this world? God no gree bad thing.

Throughout that time I was passing in the bush to Pitakwa, I did not see any sozas. I begin fear whether the fight don reach

Pitakwa at all. Because I cannot even hear the sound of gun. Any time during war if you do not see soza and you do not hear gun, you must fear. Because it means that the fight is going to start or that the fight have just finished. True, when I reach Pitakwa, I see that the fight have entered and have finished and that the people have run away again as they run away from Dukana. And as they leave everything for Dukana that is how they leave everything for Pitakwa. I know that Manmuswak and him sozas will tief everything in that town now. All those fine fine chairs, and radio and radiogram inside the house. All those fine fine things inside the shop which the people have leave and run away because they cannot stay and hear the noise of gun. I know that the sozas will tief everything and just sell them or spoil them.

And that is the exactly thing that happened. When I entered Pitakwa, I was very very hungry. I went into one of the shops. The windows and doors were all broken. Not because of the fight because I cannot see bullet mark anywhere. It is men who just broke the door and the window and entered the shop. I see plenty of things like tins of sardine and beans and all those fine fine things which fine fine people used to chop. I just take some and I chopped them. Then when night have come, I begin to go to Diobu New York to look for African Upwine Bar.

It is when I was going to that African Upwine Bar in the night that I see many many people running in the town carrying heavy heavy load for head. If you see how they are sweating and making heavy heavy noise you will know that to tief during war is not easy at all. All those heavy things as fridges and aircondition and radiogram even chairs and mattresses and beds, they were carrying them all, running up and down. I know that they cannot do all these things in the day time because if the big man of the sozas sees them, he will just shoot them one time. But they can do it in the night because then the big man soza and all his people are in their house eating and drinking and sleeping and fucking and they cannot care whether sozas are obeying the orders or not. Anyway that one is not my own palaver. My own is that I don't know where my mama and my young wife Agnes with J.J.C. have gone whether in African upwine Bar in Pitakwa or they have followed the sozas or some other people to some place where hungry is killing them. So that is the thing I was thinking of that night.

It was not hard to get to African Upwine Bar as old soza and old apprentice-driver in Pitakwa concern. All I have to do is go far away from the road-block that the sozas have made in the round-about for town. So now, I come reach the African Upwine Bar. Nobody inside at all at all. And no light sef. I come knock on the door. On all the doors. No answer. Even the whole street or even the whole Diobu. Nobody. I know say tory don *worwor*.

That night I was thinking and thinking what I will do to find my mama. I prayed to God. I was begging him to show me the way in the name of our Lord Jesus Christ Amen. So that I will know to where my mama and my wife Agnes with J.J.C. have gone to.

When day broke, you know the man I see for road walking like drunkard and belching and vomitting along the road? My master. My own master, the driver. Wonders will never end. As I see the man that early morning wonder me well well, I tell you. As the man was walking like drunkard and belching and vomitting for road surprisised me. And you know, he was wearing sozaman uniform with one rope! Well in fact another thing which surprisised me was how he recognized me when he saw me. Like say the drink just clear from his eye one time.

"Mene, my boy," he said, "what are you doing here?"

I did not waste time. I just told him all my tory because I wanted him to tell me everything that he knows about all those Dukana people who have run way from home. Chief Birabee them and all those stupid chiefs and elders. And those young young men who just like to play football in the afternoon and do not want to hear of war and gun and who will just run away from the town with the women and children into the bush or into other people country when they hear the sound of gun or if they see anybody in uniform whether the porson is worrying them or is not worrying them. So my master after he have heard my tory or sometime he did not hear my tory as he was full of drink which I think he have stolen from the shop, he just belched one big belch – "etiee" – and then he told me that all the people of Dukana have gone to camp at Nugwa.

"Gone to camp at Nugwa," I shouted. "Why camp? Are they scout or what?"

But my master did not answer another word. He just stand there begin look at me like stupid man. And I see that I cannot get anything from this man whom the war have made useless. Because you know before this war my master does not drink, he does not smoke. He was better man and very good driver. Now they have give him rope inside army and all that he is doing is to tief drink from shop and just get drunk early in the morning. So I just leave the man there to continue to vomit and belch and stagger from one side to another.

From that moment, I know that I am going to look for that camp at Nugwa. I have never heard of place called Nugwa before. When my master talk as Dukana people are making camp, to tell true I cannot understand what the man mean. So have they take all of them make scout? Are they making hut to live inside? What are they eating in that camp? I tell you I do not like the smell of this thing at all. Nevertheless I know I must go immediately to look for them.

I did not waste any time at all. I just carry my gun in my hand and walk straight away to my front. On the road, I saw one sozaman so I ask him if he know where Nugwa camp is? He just point his finger to my front. I think that sozaman is drunk too. I think all the sozas in that place have drink themself stupid with all the drink that they have tief from the shops and the houses that they have broke and entered into. Anyway that one no concern me.

I followed the road to the front. I know that since those Dukana people are not in Pitakwa and they are not in Dukana, they must be where the fighting have not reached. So I just follow as the sozaman in the lorries are going. After some time, I left the road, enter for bush. By this time all the fruits in the farms are very plenty. And even the bananas have ripe well well so I had everything that I can chop. No be hungry be de palaver. The only thing I fear is if some soza see me and dem go to tell Manmuswak and the soza captain that I am not dead but running away from the army. If that one happen, I am sure that they will catch me, put me for that Kampala, cut my tongue, cut my prick and show me pepper before they will shoot and kill me. All the time I am saying to myself, "God no gree bad thing", "God no gree bad thing."

If I tell you how I was walking in the bush for seven days and seven nights; how I was passing small small villages where all the houses have broke down and nobody living inside them; if I tell you how many ghosts I used to see in the night, it will be very very long tory. So it is not good to waste your time.

After I have gone from one broke-down village to another; after I have passed the war front and I cannot hear the sound of gun again; after I have begun to see some people all of them very thin with plenty hair like people who have never see food to chop; then after many many troubles, one day, as God used to do his things, I come see for one school compound many many lorries with sign of cross. I see one man and I ask him what they are doing in that school with many lorries and cross. He said that is it 'Red Cross Centre.' I have never heard of Red Cross Centre before so I asked him what they are doing in the Centre and whether it is Camp. He said yes, it is camp where they used to keep people who are sick from hunger and kwashiokor and who will soon die.

Kwashiokor. Kwashiokor. Kwashiokor. I am telling you, I like that name Kwashiokor. And you mean to say it is disease. If it is so, it will be a very good disease to kill somebody. Wait oh. So praps my mama and my Agnes can be suffering from this kwashiokor. Kwashiokor. When I think of that, I begin fear bad bad. So I asked the man whether that place is called Nugwa. He said that am I stupid to be asking him that kain question? Have I not been fighting in the war? Do I not know that it is not just one place that is called Nugwa? That Nugwa is a whole country and there are many towns in the country. So I asked him where the incharger of the Red Cross Centre is staying. He pointed to one place for me.

As I was going to that place, I saw one short man that I think I have seen before. This man was walking in front of me. So I walked very quickly and met him. When he heard my footstep behind, he turned and then I recognized him. It was Zaza. Zaza from Dukana. Zaza that old sozaman with him cloth who used to tell us how we have fought against Hitla in Burma. Oh I cannot tell you how my heart was beating drum – *bam* – *bam* –

bam – bam – bam. I was very happy because I think that when I have seen Zaza then I have seen all the people of Dukana with my mama and my wife Agnes among. I was really very very happy. I just hold Zaza as if he is my really brother or my really age-mate forgetting that he is many many years my senior.

Nevertheless Zaza too was very happy to see me. Although from the way he was looking at me he think that praps I am ghost because according to him they have all heard that I have already dead in the war front and it surprisised him to see me in Red Cross Centre and I am looking very strong like Burma soza of olden days.

So Zaza called me to one corner where he used to keep his clothes and he said that before I do anything or talk any talk with him, I must first of all drink and chop because he have seen many people dying with kwashiokor and influenza and I think he called another disease like hibatension and he did not want me to die like fly as everybody is dying.

So I ate and drink plenty because to talk true I was very very hungry and thirsty although I do not feel it because all I am thinking is how to find my mama and my wife Agnes with J.J.C.

So after I have eat and drink, Zaza ask me how I come reach that camp. So I told him everything from how I was fighting at Iwoama and all the things that happened to me till when Manmuswak find me for bush and take me to the hospital-school and was chooking me so that I will get well. Then I told him how they have made me soza driver and how I was able by that to go to Dukana to look for our people. When Zaza hear the name of Dukana, he cannot control himself again. Before before, he just keep quiet when I am talking. But now his eyes grew big, he opened his mouth and he held my hand. Then he said in small voice whisper:

"You actually went to Dukana?"

"Yes," is what I answered.

"Dukana still exists?"

"Sure, sure," is what I answered.

"The sozas did not destroy everything?"

"No."

"Did you see the houses?"

"Yes."

"Did you see anybody?"

"Not in the town. The people I saw were in the bush."

"In the bush!"

"Yes."

"And what were they doing in the bush?"

"Hiding."

"And who are these people?"

"Bom and Duzia."

"The two idiots. They are the one who are save. And those with safe legs and safe mind come to Nugwa to suffer and die like hen and goat and ant."

Zaza begin cry small small. Cry small small. Small small. So I asked him not to cry again but he must tell me the tory of what happened to himself and the other Dukana people. Still Zaza was crying small small, bending his head and shaking small small as he cried small small. Then after some time he told me how when the fighting began everybody was afraid.

"It was not question of old soza or not old soza. Whether Burma or no Burma. When you see death for your doormouth, you cannot wait for it to come and chop you, you fight for Burma oh, you no fight for Burma. Like when any of those big guns begin shoot, we just look for the nearby bush or lorry just put head begin dey go until we no fit hear the noise of gun again. That is how we have been running since that first day of fight near Dukana. And as the guns dey chase us that day, na so dem dey chase us till today. When we hear the gun, we just run like goat or llama. We no care where we dey go. Just dey run like foolish idiots. Na so we run sotey we come reach this Nugwa where everybody is saying na we allow the enemy to come inside Dukana and now we are inviting the enemy to Nugwa. So all the people do not want to see Dukana porson. When they ask you where you come from and you say you come from Dukana, then immediately they will ask you to leave their town. They will not give you food to eat, they will not give you water to drink, if you sick, nothing to cure you. Sozaboy, na for God hand we dey. True true. I have seen them kill and eat some Dukana people."

"Kill and eat our people?" I shouted.

"Yes, kill and eat our people."

"And these people are our friends?"

"Friends? They are not our friends. They are our worst enemy. They are worst than prison. And all those things you hear in the radio and from the D.O. who have come to Dukana before the war proper start, they are all lies. Many many lies. I think you say Duzia and Bom are still alive in Dukana?"

"Yes," is what I answered.

"You see. They are among the enemy. And they are alive and not too much worry. Nobody is running after them. But here, we are among friends and they are hunting us like anmals. I tell you, no strong young Dukana man or boy can go in this town and they will not catch him and put him in the army straight or into prison or they just kill him and eat him. Is this the action of friends?"

This is what Zaza said and then he continued; "If not for Red Cross, all Dukana people will have already dead. It is this Red Cross that goes round to collect old women and men, the children and all the sick people to put them in camp, give them food and medicine and then make sure that the cannibals do not come to kill and eat them. We have no picken now. All of them have already dead because of kwashiokor. When you see all those children with small big belly like pot, their eyes run go inside inside their head, they have begin yellow small small, Sozaboy, know that death have begin to knock for the doormouth. Kwashiokor show us pepper for one eye; our friends show us pepper for the other eye. God too far away to hear Dukana people, Sozaboy," said Zaza.

All this time, I am just wanting to ask him if he have seen my mama and my wife Agnes. But what he was telling me truly make me want to cry because I cannot know why Dukana people will suffer like say God have sent them punishment because of some bad thing that they have done before this time. So I just keep quiet and continue to listen to Zaza, old sozaman from Burma time. The only old sozaman from Dukana who have fought against Hitla. Zaza begin to shake him head and him body and I know that if not as old soza concern, he will be crying like small picken.

Then I asked Zaza if he have seen my mama and my wife Agnes. So he told me that true true he have seen them that day when everybody was running away but that he will not tell me lie that he have seen them since that day. Because in this war, everybody must find him own and praps, God will take care of all of us. But he think that some time they will be in refugee camp. This is the first time that I have heard the word and I begin to ask Zaza what it means. So Zaza said that refugee is somebody that they just throway like rubbish, no get house to stay in, no get food to eat or cloth to wear. So the camp where plenty of them are staying is like compost pit. Praps my mama and my Agnes are in one of those compost pit for porson that they have made in the bush.

Oh, I cannot tell you how this word that Zaza have said is almost driving me mad. How can my mama be in compost pit? And my young Agnes with J.J.C. So I told Zaza in strong voice that I must go and look for my young wife and my mama. And Zaza said yes, I must go because any soza who is proper soza cannot stay when all him people are missing and just answer soza for name for nothing.

So I told Zaza thank you and I say that with God's help we shall meet again for Dukana after the war have ended. Zaza say Amen but he was also shaking his head, small small. And when I asked him why he was shaking his head, he said that war is war and nobody knows what will happen tomorrow because war is war and can begin but it cannot end if it have begin. So I come shake hand with Zaza as soza and soza and I told him bye bye and I went away.

But as I was going, Zaza called me again. So I went to him. Then he asked me that what do I have in my pocket? So I told him that it is gun. And he said that I must throway the gun quick quick otherwise if any person see me holding it, they will kill me one time. And especially it is enemy gun. So I gave the gun to him, old sozaman from Burma time, and I asked him to throway it, or burn it, bend it or bury it or do anything he likes with it. And Zaza took the gun and in my very before, he just knack it for ground with force and angry many many times. The gun spoil well well. Then he just throway the gun. Then I turned and went away.

I did not look at Zaza again. It was the last time for me to see Zaza in this world.

And that is how I begin to move from one refugee camp to another to look for my mama and my young wife whom I have not seen them for almost two years now.   147

LOMBER NINETEEN

My dear brothers and sisters, I will not try to tell you how I was moving from one camp to another. Or what I saw in the camps that I went to. Because, true true as Zaza have talked, this camp is proper human compost pit and all these people they are calling refugees are actually people that they have throway like rubbish. Nothing that you can use them for. They have nothing in this world. Not common food to eat. And everything that they have, they must beg before they can get it. All their children have big big belly like pregnant woman. And if you see their eyes and legs. Just like something inside cinema or inside bad forest in dream.

I am telling you, the first time that I went inside one camp, I almost run because I think that I have reached the town of ghost, or ghost town as some people call it. I begin cry when I see all these men and women without no clothes at all, some of them with dirty dirty cloth round them waist and some with cloth full of holes. And all of them carrying small small bowl or dish waiting for small gari without no fish or meat. And not even good water to drink. And many of them sleeping on leaves of banana that they have cut because they have no mat. And all of them with long long hair because there is no barber to cut them hair and even if there is barber, where is the razor blade to use in cutting the hair of so many people? And all these people with long long hair, and big big belly, and mosquito legs, with their eyes inside inside their long long face were very many in every camp. And many of them were crying either because of sickness or hungry or because dem brother was dying and all of them with black body so, so that when you look far, it is like either bad forest in the night or like mangrove swamp when the water have gone to visit the ocean.

In fact, I do not know how I can be able to look for my Agnes and my mama inside the camp. Because those people inside the camp do not know anybody at all. If you are there, praps you will know your papa and your mama and your brother and sister, if God have helped and all of you are still together in one camp. Otherwise all these rubbish people do not know themselves. Many of them are even looking for their people and if you go and ask them whether they have seen your mama and your wife, angry and hungry will not even allow them to answer you. So all I can do is to go round and round and round looking to see if I will see my people. I will look when they are all standing in line with small small bowl in their hand waiting for the Red Cross people to give them some small food to eat. I will look when they are going to stream either to bath or to collect water for the old and sick people. I will look when they are lying down in the afternoon or in the evening. But still I cannot see my mama and my beautiful wife.

So I will leave that camp and go to another. And again na soso the same thing. Plenty people without no dress or little dress walking round with small small bowl begging for food to eat: small small picken with big belly, eyes like pit for dem head, mosquito legs and crying for food, and small yarse and waiting for death, long line of people standing, waiting for food. And still I do not see the Dukana people much less, or rather, much more my mama and my beautiful wife with J.J.C. Nevertheless you must remember that as I was going from one camp to another, I was passing the villages of the Nugwa people and I must say that what I saw in those villages can make porson cry. Because all these people cannot find food to chop. There is no fish so the people are beginning to kill and chop lizard. Oh, God no gree bad thing. To see all these men and women who are children of God killing and chopping lizard because of can't help is something that I will be remembering all the days of my life for ever and ever, amen.

It was one driver for Red Cross who told me that I have been wasting my time. That true true, if I want to find my people, I should not waste time in Nugwa. That many people do not like to stay there because of cannibals and tiefs who are plenty there. So, they all go to Urua where refugees are plenty. He said that Urua is like big city – full of *titis* and the people there are having money and they are trading as if there is no war. Believe me yours sincerely, I could not believe this thing that this driver is telling me. But still I know I must go to find out if what he is saying is true. So I went. And when I get to Urua, what I saw was actually a great surprisation to me.

If I think I have seen black forest or black swamp before, it is lie. Because the only black forest or black swamp in this world is Urua. So many people, oh God! And all of them put together in one wide open space. And some are sleeping, some are walking, some are cooking, some are drawing water, some are cutting firewood, some are wearing cloth that have tear, some have no cloth at all, many picken with big belly and mosquito legs, some picken just look like young ghost. And everybody was just talking different different language as I was going round looking and looking and asking. If I tell you that I was in that camp for one week and still I have not seen everybody, you will not believe it.

True true, this Urua is not just camp. It is new town, new dirty town born by the foolish war. And as him papa be stupid man, I know that Urua will also be stupid but you cannot just see that it is stupid town until you have lived in it for some time. Just as you will not know that war is foolish until you have fought inside it for some time and suffered as I have suffered in this foolish war that have separated me from my wife and my mama. And after one week, I am still not able to see Dukana people. In that camp, many people were trading with the enemy. They will go to where the enemy are staying to buy salt and milk and sugar and all those things and then they will come to that camp to sell it to people who have money. Always they are selling the things at very high price and those who are doing that trade are all very rich.

But one evening, I come hear some people who were singing. As you know, I am just moving from one part of that big camp to another, and I cannot move freely because it is easy for someone to say that I am deserter so I must take my time to move around in the night only and only by cunny, otherwise . . . So that evening when I was moving around again, I heard one song. I listened to it very well and I think that I have heard it somewhere before. I begin to walk to where the singing is coming from and, lo and behold, I heard the song very clearly now and I know that that song is the song of Dukana church. I think I can hear the voice of Pastor Barika as he used to shout when he is singing in the church in Dukana till you can hear his voice everywhere in Dukana every early morning throughout the whole year. So I walked quickly to join them as they are singing the song and although I no know the song well, I join them just dey shout *wa-wa-wa* as they themselves are shouting. Then after the song, Pastor Barika said everyone should close their eye. So we all closed our eye. And he prayed to God that they all want to return to Dukana and they do not want to die like ant in another man village. He said that they have suffered too much. During the war they have just been running and running in the bush and in the night and no house to sleep inside and no food to eat except what the Red Cross people are sending to them. And Pastor Barika was saying that many of Dukana people have already dead. Some of them have been killed because of hungry and others have been killed and eaten by cannibals and others have been killed by illness and some by juju and even if he is not blaming God for anything, all he is asking God is to help those who are still living and those who are sick that they will not die again. Only that they should return to Dukana. And he is also begging God to keep Dukana and their houses so that when they return they will find some place to sleep and rest and to die in peace. This is what Pastor Barika was saying in his prayer.

And I am telling you that as I was listening to Pastor Barika tears were falling from my eye. But even I was crying more when I see all those people of Dukana. True true these men were not looking like the people that I have known before. If you see how all their eyes have gone inside their head, and all their hair have become palm oil colour and they have dirty dirty rag shirt and all their bones are shaking inside their body, I am telling you, if you see all these things, and you think about them very well, you will know at once that war is a very bad and stupid game.

And when they have all said 'Amen' and opened their eye, one of those Dukana men saw me and began to shout that God have worked a new miracle. He shouted again very loud that true true God have worked a very new miracle because he have brought back one of their sons that they have think to be dead since long time when the war have just begun. "It is miracle, it is miracle," is what this man was shouting. So everyone in that place came to see me.

They were shaking hands with me or touching me for body to convince themselves that I was actually porson and myself and not spirit ghost that have just returned from burial ground. Then Pastor Barika said everyone should keep quiet. Everybody just shut up. Pastor Barika said that it is true that God is telling all the Dukana people something. And what he is telling them is that he is Jehovah and very strong Jehovah. Jehovah. Jehovah. Jehovah. The God of Abraham, of Issac and Jacob. The God of Dukana and Sozaboy. Jehovah. Jehovah.

"My dear brothers and sisters of Dukana, as God saved his people before, that is how he is going to save all of us. Look at this our son and brother, Sozaboy, did we not all think that he have already dead? Yet here we see him. Stronger and bigger than before before. God is wonderful. Let us all trust him. Let us be patient. Let us pray."

And Pastor Barika began to thank God how he have saved and redeemed his people and helped to deliver them from the land of Egypt to promised land which is Canaan and now he have brought back Sozaboy from the land of spirit in the same way as he have brought back Lazarus from hell. Then he come beg God that after all we know that hell is the place where bad porson used to go after he have already dead. But this one that Dukana people are inside is more than hell sef although there is no fire burning all the time. He said that if there is anything that Dukana people have done which is annoying God, he should forgive them because they have already suffered enough and in fact all those people who have already dead in this war have used their blood to suffer for all those who are still alive. Then he said Allelu! and all the people answered Alleluya! And again 'Allelu!' and all the people answered 'Alleluya'.

So after this prayer, Chief Birabee and Pastor Barika took

me away to their hut inside inside the camp. I am telling you that when I see where these people are living, I was very ashamed and angry. Because even rat sef cannot live like this. I think you understand. If sozaman live like rat inside pit in the bush waiting for enemy, that is fine. Because sozaman life is nonsense and rubbish. Sozaman can die at any time. Na him choose him choice. But how can big man who is chief and having five or six wives and Pastor who is man of God live in this kind of place? Real bush. All they have done is to clear the bush and put some dirty dirty rag cloth for ground. And that is their bed. And if it rain, the leaves and palm frond that they have used to cover the hut roof cannot stop the rain from reaching their body. True true these men are just living like anmal. And because why? Yes, that is what I was asking myself. Because why? That foolish man Chief Commander General have told lie about enemy and no enemy. But was it not the enemy that saved my life? And all those Dukana people who have already dead, is it enemy that killed them? Is it not that foolish Chief Commander General who told his sozas to remove these Dukana people from their village? Is it not so? So all this suffering is total useless. And to fight war is even more useless.

This is what I was thinking as I sat inside that hut with Chief Birabee and Pastor Barika. And believe me yours sincerely tears were falling down from my eyes like rain. But when I see that Chief Birabee and Pastor Barika are looking at me one kain one kain, I just stopped crying. So after I have stopped now, Pastor Barika asked me to tell them how I have reached that place. So I told them about the things that have happened to me. You know that I cannot tell them everything from A to Z. I just tell them some of the things that they will like to hear. Because they are old men and you cannot treat old men bad bad. But I come spend long time on how I got to Dukana and found Bom and Duzia sitting down to drink palm wine and eating all the plantain and yam in Dukana because everyone have gone away and no one in the village. I told them that although some of the houses are still standing, many others have fallen because of no one to take care of them. I told them that it is because I cannot find my people that I decided to go and look for them. Because I think that if I see all or many Dukana people in one place, then surely my mama and my wife can fit to be there.

So Pastor Barika told me that my mama and my wife are not in that camp. That he does not think that they are near that camp sef. Because he have seen some soza captains taking them away in a lorry. He think that because my Agnes is very beautiful gal, sometimes the sozaman will take her and take very good care of her and my mama.

I no like this thing that Pastor Barika is saying, oh. What does he mean? Take good care of Agnes because she is beautiful gal. What type of care is that? Anyway, I don't want to talk to this Pastor Barika. So I no answer am.

Then Chief Birabee asked me if I am still soza. I told him that once a soza always a soza. So he asked whether I will still carry gun and fight. And I said that what is very very important to me now is to know where my mama and my Agnes are hiding or staying, not fighting useless fight. Chief Birabee and Pastor come look at themselves with one kain eye. Then Chief Birabee said that it is good for everybody to join in the fighting. Because it is war that we must win.

I did not like how this Chief Birabee was talking, you know. What does he mean by 'war that we must win'? So all this suffering and dying have not make any difference at all to the old man? He is still the same stupid old chief that he was in Dukana. Just fearing any stranger that comes from government or anybody who says that government have sent him to work in Dukana or to tell him some word.

As soza concern, I know that I must to be careful in front of this Pastor and Chief. So I told them that as night is coming, I must go and look for some place to sleep. They said to me that I can sleep in their hut. I said thank you because as a sozaboy, I know what to do when things are hard. So Pastor Barika told me to go away and take care of everybody and not just think and think and talk and talk of my mama and my wife. Because everyone is equal in the eye of God. And Chief Birabee said that I should remember that all young men are wanted to go and fight in the front so that the enemy can be defeated and we win the war and then we shall all return home and we shall be in a new country where nobody will tief, there will be no hungry again, everything will be free, from water to food, to cloth to wear to medicine to lorry and licence. And nobody will take bribe again and everyday the sun will shine long time and the rain will fall short time and the yam and maize will grow well well and everyone will get work or anything that the person want to do he can do. In short, after we have win the war, there will be life more abundant. So I asked myself that if we do not win the war then what will happen?

So I thanked the Pastor and Chief and I walked out of their hut. I was not happy as I was leaving that hut. Because I do not like how the Chief and the Pastor were looking at themselves when I say I do not like to fight useless fight. And I do not like how they are saying that everything will be very nice if we win the war. Is it possible? How can?

By this time, they were ringing the bell. It was chop time. Everyone was running towards the place where they are cooking. Then they will all stand in line and hold their plate in their hand. Then the cooks will put some food inside the plate. I can see that they are all fighting for the food. Because nobody like to stand behind the other one in the line. Everybody want to go first should in case the food should finish quick quick. Oh, I was really sorry when I see good man like Terr Kole struggling with young man, old woman, small picken for sake of small food to chop. So I told Terr Kole that he should not stand in the line. That I will get the food for him. Terr Kole allowed me to get the food and he was waiting when I returned.

He said that he will not go to his hut because there are very many people there and he wants to tell me something very important. So we went to near the bush where nobody was near us and nobody can hear what we are saying. Then he chopped that his chop. It was very small and I know that even dog will not be satisfy with that chop. But that was all everybody can find to eat. Terr Kole said that they used to eat like that once a day. Unless the white woman from Red Cross come to the camp then they can eat two times for that day. But if not, it is only once a day for all the people.

"Do you hear me, Sozaboy," is what Terr Kole said. "It is like that for many people. But there are some people, few people who are eating very well. Three times a day. Those few people and all their family. Those people are also having plenty money. I do not know what they will use all the money for. But they hide the money under the ground for the same place where they bury all those small small children who are dying because of hungry and kwashiokor." This is what Terr Kole said as he was cleaning his finger with his tongue like say he does not want any part of the chop to loss.

Terr Kole said that he does not want to call anybody name. But some people have chopped the people food and sold the cloth that the Red Cross people ask them to give all the people. They are selling this food and cloth and afterwards they will preach to the people and when they have dead because of hungry, they will bury them with big prayer and ask God to take care of them in heaven. Terr Kole said that he is not blaming anybody, oh. But he have to say that the camp where Dukana people are staying is not good for anybody who is somebody. He said that it is very bad for young man. Because some people have sold their eyes and their ears to the big sozas for their belly. He said that these people have big big belly, big big ear, big big nose and big big eyes. They see everything. They smell everything. And they hear everything. So they chop everything. Because they want to chop for today, tomorrow and even for many tomorrows to come, they even hear things which nobody have said, they see things which their belly told them to see and they smell things according to how their belly tell them to smell. So these bellymen are friends of the sozas and of the politicians and the traders. And they are all trading in the life of men and women and children. And their customer is death.

So Terr Kole told me that because he likes me, he will tell me to return to Dukana as I am good young man and can know my way and road to Dukana. Terr Kole told me that he does not think that my mama and Agnes are in trouble. That true true since they left Dukana he have not seen them in the *ye-ye* camps that Dukana people have been staying inside. So he thinks that by God's help they will return to Dukana. He said it is more important that young man like myself should be in Dukana so that the town will not die than stay in this camp or go to the war front again. And Terr Kole laughed small small, small small. He said that war is another queer thing. That when war is happening we cannot trust anybody, even ourself. So he said I must to be careful. And not to tell what he have told me to anybody. I wanted to tell him what Pastor and Chief have told me before. But Terr Kole put his finger on my mouth. He told me not to tell him any tory because he know what he knows as old man concern. That he is not picken and he did not buy his white hair for market. Then he told me to go away that I should try and sleep well. I told him thank you and I went away.

By this time night have come well well. And in all that camp there was no noise at all. It is like all the Dukana people are like beetles fighting slow slow with one big piece of smelling shit. I think that all these people who are very hungry just cannot sleep at all. And myself all the things that Terr Kole have told me is worrying me bad bad. Plus when I think of Chief Birabee and Pastor Barika, I know that something very very bad is happening in that camp. And to tell you the truth, I did not sleep the whole of that night.

There were many many things I was thinking. First that soza captain who gave Bullet urine to drink, then Manmuswak who gave us cigar and hot drink and then killed our people and then he was chooking me to make me live again, then Dukana without goat and chicken and people and now this rotten rubbish human compost pit that they are calling refugee camp. And my mama and my young wife Agnes with J.J.C.

So as I was lying down on the ground and looking into that black night, the only question I ask myself is 'which one I dey?' 'Which one be my own?'

LOMBER TWENTY

In the morning when I woke up, in front of me, lo and behold, there was one big man standing. He told me to follow him one time, no question. I just followed him like goat. Because I know that war is war and anything can happen and that is that. So I followed the man like goat. As he was walking in front of me, I can see that the man fit be soza. Because his leg is very strong and he is walking very fast. All the Dukana people in that camp were looking at me and some of them were just shaking their head small small, small small. Then I begin to think that some bad thing will soon happen. And the man who have called me was still walking and walking till we reached that place where Pastor Barika and Chief Birabee were staying. Then the man asked me to stand in front of the both men as they were sitting in their hut. It is only when I look carefully that I see what I have not seen before. On the other side, or what am I saying, behind the hut, there are many bags of gari, rice and bundles of stockfish. Plenty of them. And then I look at Barika and Birabee well well. The two of them are very fat like pig. All this one that the Dukana people are thin and hungry no reach those two men. It was that time that I remembered what Terr Kole said as how these men can sell their children so that they will eat plenty of food when other people are suffering.

Nevertheless, as I was standing there, the man asked Chief Birabee whether he have known me before in Dukana. Chief Birabee said yes. He asked him whether I am soza before. Chief Birabee said yes, I am soza in enemy army before. I tell you, I just wan piss for my trousers because I know what it means to be enemy soza. And if the Chief of your town tell the big big sozas that kain thing, you must know that they will kill you sef.

So I just begin to run one time. I run without looking the place I am going. I just run like mad. And as I run, the man who have called me run after me. Some Dukana people just follow the man to pursue me. They followed me shouting and shouting until they catch me. Then they gave me to the man. The man just tie my hand behind my back and asked me to go in front of him. That as I am a good runner, I must run today till I see pepper. He said that he is going to take me to his *oga* and that one will say what they will do to me. So as I walked in front of him with my hand tied behind my back, he started beating me with stick. Every time he beat me with that stick, I think that I am going to die. But the beating that they are beating me is nothing because, true true as the man talk, the running that I was going to run is even worse.

Now when we come reach the man land rover because he is driving land rover, he just tied my hand with rope to the land rover just as the people used to tie goat that they are taking to the market to sell. Then he went inside the land rover and kicked the car. The engine started. I think that he will come and throw me into the back of the land rover like goat that they are taking to slaughter house in Pitakwa to kill. Not at all. The man just begin to move the land rover, small small, small small. Then the rope begin to pull me. I followed the rope. The motor was going and I was following. Inside hole, on bad road, on coal tar, on dirty road, I was just following the rope that was tied behind the car, running and running and running. Oh Jesu. The motor was going and I was following, running. And I was tired, oh God. And I could not even talk or cry. After some time, I will fall and roll on the ground. But the land rover will not slow down. I will just roll on the ground and follow like dog that have already dead. And the land rover will be speeding proper proper. I said to myself, 'Sozaboy, you don die well well today.' We were going like that and my head was turning and turning until I do not know what have happened to me.

When I opened my eyes, I cannot see anything. I think I was in cave or hole for rabbit or something like that because it was very very dark. And all my body was paining me. I cannot carry my hand up. And my leg is like big big load. My head was full of wound as I can feel it. And oh, I just want to die because the pain was too plenty. I begin cry small small, small small. Until I don't know what happened again.

When I opened my eyes again, it is still the same thing. My head was beating drum, beating drum, beating drum. And I cannot carry up my hand or leg. And all my body was full of wound and my belly was turning and turning and turning. Even I cannot cry sef. And I just think I must die, die one time. Because it is better to die and buried than to live like maggot as I am living now. I was asking God to take my life one time. Then I will just close my eye and will not know what have happened again.

It was like this for long long time. I cannot tell you how long time it is because I do not know how many years have passed since they threw me into that cave or rabbit hole. And I was sleeping and waking, sleeping and waking, all that time, with my head beating drum and I was hearing plenty shout like train, motor, aeroplane and motor cycle passing inside my ear all the time that I am awake.

Then one time, somebody come open the door and I see the light as I was lying on the floor. The man say I should get up. I just don't know what he wants me to do because my leg is very heavy. He began to shout that I should get up now now. And since I cannot do so by myself, he just pulled my hand with force. I got up and then I fell again like bag for one corner. Then he called some more people to come and carry me. They carried me outside. Then I see that I am in some kain Army Camp again. Plenty sozas walking up and down and running up and down. And plenty people like myself without shirt only pant with wound for all dem body.

So one of the sozas told me that I am enemy soza and I must be buried alive. I just hear the man. I don't know what he is talking about. I just see his lips move up and down, up and down. Then he told the sozas who have carried me from the room to throw me inside land rover and take me away. I think that true true they are going to take me away to bury me alive. So I just fall down like a bag of gari. The sozas carry me one time, throw me inside the land rover and drove away.

I don't know where they are taking me to. I was inside that land rover for a very long time. And all that time, my head was paining me bad bad. Oh I tell you, I was very very sick. I hear many people shouting and laughing inside my head. Then we got to another Army camp and the land rover stopped. So they took me from the land rover and threw me inside another room. This time, not me alone dey for the room. Plenty of us. And I can tell you that that room was smelling bad bad with shit and urine.

After I have stayed in that prison for some time, my eye begin clear small small. The pain for my body and inside my head was not plenty again. I begin to talk to the porson who was sitting near me. I begin to feel hungry and thirsty. So I just asked the porson who is near me whether he can give me water to drink and some food to chop. He said that he is prisoner of war like myself. That he have no food and no water. That since he came to that prison, they have not given him any food. Only palm kernel and dirty water every afternoon. That they will soon come and bring the palm kernel and dirty water for that day. And true true after some time, one porson brought it. He called it ration. I was very hungry and thirsty. So I drank the water and ate the palm kernel. Everything tasted very very nice. And then I come sleep again.

When I woke up, I was still feeling pain in my leg and my body. But my head don clear well well. Just suddenly, I begin remember all the things that have happened to me since that time that I was standing in front of Chief Birabee and Pastor Barika. And all the bad things that have happened to me since. Then I come remember my mama and my wife, Agnes. And I say to myself that I must escape from that prison. Because should in case I cannot escape, then I will not see my people again. And I have promised myself that I must see them in this world before I die. When I was thinking like this, one tall man came and called one of the prisoners. The prisoner went out with him. Although that prison was very dark, because of no light, I think that I have seen that tall man before. I think that I have heard that voice before.

Next day, after they have brought us the palm kernel and the dirty water, the tall man came in again and called another prisoner. The prisoner went out with him. It was that time that I asked the prisoner who was lying near to me where they were taking the prisoners to. He told me that he thinks they will either shoot them or bury them alive. Because any time they took away a prisoner, they do not bring him back again. Only after some time, we will hear the sound of one shot of gun and that will be all. He said that they do not ask anybody any question. They will just shoot you or bury you alive. Unless everybody was busy fighting that particular day, then they will forget to kill the prisoner. Otherwise because they have no food to give the prisoners and no cloth and no medicine and no anything, it is better to kill the prisoners.

"Why do they not kill all the prisoners one time and even before they put them in prison?" I asked the prisoner.

"Praps they have no ammo to use in killing the prisoner. Or praps the prisoner is too weak or tired or ill to dig his grave," the prisoner replied.

"So that is how they will call us one by one?" I asked.

"Oh yes," the prisoner said. 'It is turn by turn."

"Do you know when it will be your turn?"

"Any time from now."

"And are you ready to die?"

"Sure. Is a matter of can't help," the prisoner replied.

Chei! You see how this prisoner is talking about death as if it is nothing to him, as if it is play or something like that.

"Have you been in this prison for long time?" I asked.

"No. They just captured me in war front. I have been here for seven days."

"Seven days!"

"Yes. And every day, they are shooting one one prisoner. But they must hurry up if they want to kill all the prisoners because the war will soon end."

"Is it so?"

"Oh yes. The war will soon end. Our people are pressing on. They will smash these people very soon."

"True?"

"Oh yes. The war will soon end. And all sozas can then return home. Pity I will not be there when it's all over. But no regret."

162

As this soza was talking was a great surprisation to me. Nothing was worrying him at all at all. He was just talking like porson who is inside his own house and preparing to go to have his bath or eat his food.

"Do you have wife and picken and mama?"

"Oh yes."

"Do you not like to see them again?"

"If God permit. If not, then that is that."

"Have you been soza for long time?"

"Since the war began. Not very long. I joined the army because I like as the sozas were marching and singing and wearing fine fine uniform and boot. The one I like most is the cap. Even for that cap alone, I can join army one hundred times."

"And have you enjoyed to be soza?" I asked him.

"Oh yes. A soza's life is a merry one."

"So does it mean you enjoy to be prisoner like this?"

"Oh no."

"Then why have you not run away from this prison?"

"Because I cannot run away."

"And will it pain you when they call you to shoot you or bury you alive?"

"It is soza's life. Nobody can run away from death. After all some people die in their sleep. Old men can die and small picken can die. A sozaman and death are brothers."

I was looking at this soza prisoner with my mouth open very wide. Because as you know, I am worrying plenty about how they are going to shoot me or bury me alive and I will not see my mama and Agnes with J.J.C. again. But he is not worrying about anything at all. Or is he?

"So you are not worrying about anything at all?" I asked him.

"My only worry is that I did not have enough ammo to kill myself that day I was captured in war front. What I wanted to do was to kill the enemy and then use the last bullet to kill myself before anyone can make me a prisoner. But man proposes and God disposes. That is why they were able to catch me that day. However, I have no regret because war is war."

Aha, this soza prisoner have said that thing again. War is

war. When I hear that word again, I begin to think of all the things that have happened to me since I was in Dukana, till I come join the enemy army and go to Dukana to see all those broken down houses and how my Agnes and my mama are missing and all those suffering in the refugee camp and how they have now taken me to be prisoner and they can shoot me or bury me alive and nobody will know or care because after all there are so many people dying in the war front and so many who are dying in prison or refugee camp and that is that. And when I think of Manmuswak that I have seen in African Upwine Bar in New York Diobu and then in war front and now this soza prisoner who does not worry whether he will die or not, I begin to know that after all I am not small boy again. That I cannot keep on thinking of my mama and Agnes because the other things that I am seeing in this war are even more important than anything that can happen to me or to my family. I begin to think that the world is not a good place even. That if porson die, it is better for that porson than to continue to live in this wicked world. So praps Bullet is now resting in peace as they used to say, and nobody can give him urine to drink or put him in prison and beat him then bury him alive. I think that praps if I die that day when the bombs were falling at Iwoama or even that time it was raining, that I will be happy by now. Because I will not live to see that Chief Birabee and Pastor Barika calling sozas to come and arrest me and put me in prison and kill me because I am enemy soza and because when they have told the sozas about me they will get some rice and stockfish and rag clothes for demself and their family.

But as I was thinking this, I said no. Because anyone who have seen my wife Agnes and J.J.C. must like such good thing. And it is not good for young man to die when he have not enjoyed and he have not done anything that he can show to his children and his mama. And after all the world is very nice place with very many nice things that God have made for enjoyment of man and there is no need for man to die just like that like ant or goat or chicken. So I said that no, I must not die because I have to wait and see the end of the war and become big man with my own car and plenty of money and big house and very very fine things and I will show that Chief Birabee and

Pastor Barika pepper because of what they have done to me and all the Dukana men and women who are dying in refugee camp because of hunger and kwashiokor. Nevertheless I can see myself as very rich man with very big belly and walking all over Dukana and everyone will be following me asking me for help to send their picken to school and for money so that they can buy food to eat. And they will be begging me to allow them sweep my house or be apprentice in my lorry or driver. And I will be driving away those that I do not like while I will give some fine things to those that I like and everyone will be talking about me how I am a good man to those who are good and bad to those who are bad.

So I was thinking all these things for some time and I did not speak to the soza prisoner. After now, I looked for him to ask him some question, but he have gone away to another part of the room where he is talking with another prisoner. Then afterwards, he returned. So I asked him where he have gone.

"I think the war is about to end," he said.

"About to end? How do you know? Are you not in this prison with us? How can you hear something like that?"

"I am old soza, my friend. We know what we know. I am sure that the war will soon end if it have not ended already."

"Did you hear about it in radio or what?" I asked.

"Do not worry. We know what we know."

"So what will happen to us?" I asked again.

"I do not know. Praps they will set us free. Praps they will come and kill us all one time. Everything is in the hand of God. Because war is war. Anything can happen."

So I was happy small because the war will soon end. And I was begging God to not allow those sozas to kill me because I want to find out what have happened to my people. I am sure that if the war end and my people are still alive, they must return home to Dukana. As I was begging God like this, suddenly the door of the prison was opened with loud noise and they asked everybody to go out. I saw that soza prisoner who was talking to me with confidence jump up quick quick and he ran quick quick to the man who have opened the door of the prison with loud noise and he put his hand in his knicker and gave the man something and the man allowed him to go away quick quick as if he is not prisoner again. *Shoo*!

Meanwhile, the rest of us begin to walk small small as sick man or prisoner concern. There was plenty of noise outside, the noise of gun and ammo which are not very far away and trucks and motors moving and sozas who are running and shouting. In short, everything was confused. The sun was shining inside my eye and I covered my face with my hand. Immediately, one man came and beat my hand down and told me don't be stupid. He was very tall man and I looked at him well. Immediately, I saw that it is Manmuswak. Yes, it is Manmuswak. It is Manmuswak that I have seen open the door the first time; it is Manmuswak that have taken something from that soza and allowed him to go away and now it is Manmuswak that is beating my hand down and asking me to don't be stupid. Wonders will never end. Wonders will never end. I think you remember that the first time I saw this Manmuswak is at the African Upwine Bar when he was chopping stockfish and drinking palmy and telling that his friend the short man that he can fight any war if they tell him to fight it. Then the next time he was with enemy at Iwoama giving us drink and cigar before the bomb begin to fall. And the next time he was chooking me injection in that school hospital and using me to make driver of land rover. And now this Manmuswak is again with our own sozas and no longer with enemy sozas. Or *abi* na which side the man dey now? At first I could not believe my eyes because I cannot understand how this Manmuswak can be fighting on two sides of the same war. Is it possible? Or is it his brother? Or are my eyes deceiving me because I am sick since a long time? Or is it ghost I am seeing? True true my eye cannot deceive me, I am telling you. This man is Manmuswak. I see the way that he is walking and his long legs and coconut head and I am quite sure he is Manmuswak. But if he is Manmuswak then he must remember me because after all I have been his driver for some time.

After he pulled down my hand from my face, he began to shout and say that we are all prisoners and enemy sozas and deserters and he have orders to shoot all of us before the war end and before the enemy reaches our camp. Because there is no food for us to eat and no lorry to take us out of that prison, and after all we are prisoners and he can kill any useless prisoner who is not better than maggot. So I tried to make him know that I am Sozaboy that he have saved in that school hospital. But Manmuswak eye was red like pepper. He does not look at me or listen to me at all and all the time he was just shouting and telling all of us to march forward, left, right, left, right, left, right, halt. So now we all marched forward. No one said even one word. We all marched till we got near the bush. Then he asked all of us to stand in straight line.

When we have all stood in straight line, he walked and stood in front of us. True true, I thought the man was joking. Then he pulled the gun and began to shoot. The prisoners were falling one after the other. One, two, three, four, five, six, seven. I close my eye and pray to God that he will take care of my mama and my young wife Agnes. As for myself, well, it is sozaman life to die anytime. But I was fearing. Still, Manmuswak was shooting. And the prisoners were falling. Plenty blood. Plenty blood and plenty shout. Then I heard Manmuswak say, "oh God, no more ammo." When I heard that, I just opened my eyes. And I saw Manmuswak throw down his gun and then make sign of the cross and run away. Still about two prisoners that he have not killed plus myself.

Immediately, we three just run into the bush.

LOMBER TWENTY-ONE

I think you know I was not very strong. So I stopped inside the bush after some time. All the time, I was hearing the sound of gun. And then night come fall. I slept that night like no man business, although many time, I will just wake up thinking that Manmuswak have found ammo and he is coming to look for we three that he have not killed before. Then I will look round and there is no Manmuswak and then I will sleep again. Then when day come broke and I come open my eye well well, no sound of gun again. I was still lying inside the bush because I do not know what have happened. And I am waiting to see whether I will find someone who will tell me something about anything.

As you know, since they catch me for that refugee camp, I do not know anything about anything. But I do not see or hear anybody. All the time, the thing that appeared for my eye is Manmuswak as he was shooting the prisoners standing in line. And all those young men just looking at the gun as Manmuswak is firing. And I am asking myself how the ammo just finish for Manmuswak gun like say someone send am message. And if the ammo did not finish like that, by now I would have already dead, and that will be that.

So I begin to think of all those prisoners that Manmuswak have killed, how all of them are falling down and shouting and no one to bury them. And by now vultures will begin to chook their eyes and to chop them one by one, and ant too plus maggot. Man picken! I don't think I can forget for the rest of my life how all those men were standing in one line and the bullets just going inside them one by one and they were just falling down on top of each other and all their blood was running together like stream, I think. And how can we know what those people did? Some times they are just innocent people like myself and now they have already dead because of nonsense war. I begin to think that I will go back to that place to see what have happened to all of them. I want to know because sometimes one or two of them have not dead and if possible I can fit to help them.

But just as I was thinking of this, then I heard people shouting. I listened carefully. They were saying that the war have ended. That everyone should return from the bush and wherever they are hiding. That there will be no more shooting of gun, no more prisoner of war for sozas and everyone can go to his village because everything is awright now. To tell you true, I cannot believe all this at first because I cannot understand how the fighting will just stop automatic like that. Only yesterday Manmuswak was shooting prisoners and today they are telling us that the war have ended. Some time it is just trick so that porson will commot from the bush and then they will arrest him and shoot him. Because it is possible that there are many people like Manmuswak who are just liking to kill and such porson will do anything to kill whether soza or civilian because to him war is war and anything can happen and whether people die or they do not die is not his own concern.

So although I have heard that the war have ended and that we should all commot from the bush, I still remain there. Because by this time, I am no longer afraid of bush as I have stayed inside bush at Iwoama and inside bush the time I was going to look for Agnes my wife and my mama inside all those refugee camps. Then after two nights and two days and true true I do not hear the sound of gun again, only birds singing in the tree for morning time and in the night just cricket making noise, I think that true true praps the war have ended and that it is time to return to Dukana. If so, all those Dukana people will now go back and some time my mama and my wife Agnes will be there too.

It was when I began to think of my wife and my mama that I

just tell myself that I will not hide inside that bush again. I must return quick quick to Dukana. If possible, I will go to that camp where all the Dukana people were staying and some time I will be able to see my mama. So I come commot from that bush. And when I got to the road, I saw many many people with load on their head just walking in one line from where I was standing till I cannot see again either for my right hand or for my left hand. In short all the people when the war have ended were returning to their village and because there is no motor to carry them and also the people have no money, they were just walking by leg and carrying their small load on their head.

Believe me yours sincerely, if you see as those people were looking, you will sorry for them. Everyone very black and dirty with rag cloth for body or sometime no cloth at all sef, and the things they are carrying on the head like small bundle also very dirty and like rag and all the men and women and children very thin and some of them with big big belly and brown hair on their head. They were all walking, walking, walking very very slow because you can see that they are tired and have no power again. Even some of them just drop for ground as they are walking and die. Then their friend or brother will stop and make small pit and bury the man or woman and then they will carry their small rag bundle again and continue to go as they were going before. They cannot even cry for the porson who have dead.

Nevertheless, I myself joined them to walk. At first, I do not know where to go because I do not know where I am. After some time, I come meet one sozaman and I come ask am where is Pitakwa. Then he pointed to where the sun is rising and I begin to walk in that direction. I walked for very very long time. The whole of that day in fact. All the time what I was seeing was long long lines of men and women and children either walking the same road as myself or passing me in the other direction. All of them have small bundle for hand and nobody was talking because they are not strong enough to talk. Many times, I will pass some villages. All the houses in the village have either fallen down or some part of it have fallen down. And then I will see some men and women just sitting down in front of the house either crying or putting their head in their hand. Some people are clearing the ground to remove all the weed and grass that have started to grow outside and inside the house. It was not a good thing to see at all at all.

I continued to walk like that for three days and three nights before I can get to Pitakwa. When I got to Pitakwa, I can see that a lot of people have returned to the town. There is plenty of noise but not as before. People are riding bicycle, but not too many. As for motor, many of them have broke down and no one to repair. So the people who are returning to the villages near Pitakwa are all walking in straight line too with small small bundle in their hand or on their head. I think that as I am very near to Dukana now that praps I will see some Dukana people and may be my mama and my Agnes. But although I waited and looked for long time for that place, I did not see any Dukana people at all. So I knew that I must walk to Dukana and by God's help when I get there, I will see everyone who have fit able to return.

After another one day and one night, I come reach Dukana. As I was getting to the forest which is in front of my home town, my heart was beating drum – *dam dim dam dim dam dim dam, dam dim dim.* Because I do not know what is waiting for me. I am begging God please to allow me to see my mama and my Agnes again. I am asking whether Agnes is still young good wife with J.J.C. or whether one sozaman have taken her away from me and I will not see her again or even if I see her, she will not be my wife again. I am wondering if that foolish Chief Birabee and wicked Pastor Barika are still alive and whether they have returned to Dukana to play their wickedness again. I am saying to myself that if I see them I will tell them something because of the way they have handed me to those sozas to beat me and kill me just because I am looking for my family and I do not want to fight useless war again. I say to myself that I must tell all the Dukana people how those people are useless and nobody should go to church and listen to Pastor Barika because he can sell his mama sake of money and all the preaching that he have been preaching in Dukana is all lies. And I am thinking how when I see my mama sometime she will not fit to be able to recognise me, but I will go to her and tell her that I am her son and I am sorry how I have disobeyed her word not to join army because I have seen now that army is useless and war is even more useless and that from this time I will be very good man and fine driver. And she will just cry and be very happy that I have returned to Dukana. And she will show me where my wife Agnes is standing waiting for me to hold her and embrace her. Oh, I think it will be wonderful.

So now, I come enter the village. It surprised me that every place was very very quiet. Ah-ah. Have the people of Dukana not returned from the war? From refugee camp? From compost pit camp? Or have they all dead from hunger and kwashiokor? Or what is happening?

I come walk more and more into the village. Every place was still very quiet, and all the houses that have broken down nobody have repaired them. And there was plenty grass everywhere. More than the other time that I have come to Dukana before I went to look for my people. Wonderful. My heart begin to cut well well. I begin fear that I will not see my mama and my Agnes again. I continued to walk. I think you know that by this time, the sun have begin to go down and night was coming. But porson can still see everything oh. It was not yet night. I walk quick quick, quick quick to where my mama house used to be. When I got there now, the house cannot be seen at all. Even the thatch was not there again. No sign that house was in that place. Ah-ah. What does this mean? And I cannot see anybody at all. Wonders will never end. So I begin to go to some house that I have seen but I have not looked carefully.

As I was getting near that house, one woman come commot from inside. I was walking towards her, and she just stood there, looking at me, looking at me. I called her because I know her name. She just stayed in that front of her house and looked at me. And when I walked to her to get near her, she just jumped up, ran inside the house with fear and closed the door. When I knock for the house, I no hear any reply at all. I knock and call my name plenty times but still no answer.

So I come go another house in the village. Everybody have closed their door and they are inside the house. Every time that I knock on the door, they will go and open the door. But as soon as they see me, they will just shout and enter the house and lock the door. And even if I stay there and shout my name one hundred times and beg that all I want to know is if my mama or my Agnes is in that house or any other house for Dukana or anywhere in this world at all, nobody will answer me. Everywhere that I go to it was the same thing.

So as night was coming to fall now, I just go inside the broken church because that is the only building that is still standing and the doors are open and I think that nobody will throw me out of it because after all it is the house of God and all of us are God's picken although that Pastor Barika is the in-charger of the church and he is very wicked man.

So that night, I lay inside the church. If I tell you that I sleep well, I am telling lie and God will punish me. Because all the time, what I am wondering is where my mama and my wife are staying. And then, why is everybody running from me as soon as they hear my voice or my name? And why is Dukana still like village where all the people have already dead? Do they know that the war have ended? These are the questions I was asking myself and I could not sleep throughout that night.

During that night, I heard some people who are crying small small, small small. I looked from the door of the church where I was staying and I saw some people moving, holding one small lantern. I moved small out of the church so that I can see them proper and hear them well well. They were walking, carrying one small bundle and crying. I followed them. They were walking to the forest which as you know is very very near the town. I followed them. After some time when they are in the beginning of the forest, they stopped. I myself stopped too and I went to hide behind one small bush so that they will not see me. Because they are holding lantern, I myself can see everything that they are doing. Then they kept the small bundle down. And one man took a hoe that he was carrying and begin to dig the ground. He was digging, digging, digging and the other people were crying, crying. After he have dig for some time and made hole in the ground they put the bundle inside the ground and covered the hole that they have dig with soil. Then they begin to cry again, small small, small small. Hardly sef that I can hear them. Then they carried their lantern again and begin to go back where they have come from.

I myself followed them. And when I get near the church, I entered the church again. Every place was very very dark. There is no noise in Dukana at all. No noise at all. I begin to turn for my mind what I have seen. As you know, when somebody die in Dukana, they have to cry plenty and drink plenty *ginkana*, *push-me-I-push-you*, and they will bury the porson after three days or so. But even when they have buried him, they will still cry and drink and dance. That is if the porson is good man and he just died. They will always bury him in his house whether inside or in his compound. But if the porson have died by juju or some bad illness, that man or woman will not be buried inside his house or inside the village. He must be buried in the bad forest so that the bad thing that have killed him will not stay in the town and begin to kill more and more people. And nobody can cry for anybody who have died from juju. Because if anybody cries for that porson who have been killed by juju it means that the porson who is crying knows about the juju or praps he is the messenger of the juju and he can kill other people too in the village.

So when I saw those people carrying that small bundle to the forest and digging the ground, I know that bad porson have died and that something bad is happening. But I was not surprised plenty. Because after all it is not first time that juju have killed somebody in Dukana.

But in fact what began to worry me is that after some time that night, I see another people with lantern and small bundle going to the bad forest. I followed them too and I saw them as they were digging the ground and burying the small bundle that they were carrying on their head and they were crying small small, small small, after that. And every time I will return to the church and wait and then they will come again with small bundle and lantern always going to the bad forest. So I knew that some bad thing is happening in Dukana.

True true, something bad is happening. That is why nobody agreed to open the door for me even though I was shouting my name. Praps that is why when they see me they just run inside the house and close the door. Then fear come catch me. So that night, I did not sleep at all.

Early in the morning after the second cock crow I was

thinking that praps people will come to the church. But there was no bell. And no church. Nobody moving around in Dukana sef as they used to do before, either to go to the farm or to go and fish or to draw water from the stream. So everybody is just staying inside their house and locking the door. Wonderful. Something very bad is happening in this Dukana, that is what I was saying to myself. And I begin to sorry for myself. Because even in my own town I have no house, I am staying inside the church and nobody can agree to put me inside their house or even open the door for me. When they hear my voice or my name they will just close the door and run away. And no news of my mama or my Agnes. Oh God, what have I done to suffer like this? Ehn? What have I done that you are punishing me?

After now, when day have broke well well, I am very confused. I don't know whether I will go outside that church or whether to stay inside or whether to go away from Dukana or what to do. So I said I will wait inside the church for some time and see whether some people will go out of their house and then praps I can ask them what is happening in Dukana. But for very long time nobody came out of their house. Every place was just very quiet. Then I myself said no, I cannot stay inside that church. After all am I not sozaboy? Can I be fearing anything after what I have seen as soza in Iwoama and in war front and in prison camp? Can I be fearing? Why? I must go and shake all those Dukana people who are hiding in their house. Praps they are still thinking that the war have not finished. If so, I will go and tell all of them that the war have already end and surely as I am sozaboy they will listen to me and stop their fear and behaving like cockroach that is hiding in dark corner of the house when day have broke.

So I come get out of that church and begin to walk. First I went to where our house used to stand. And true true there was no house. Same as yesterday. So my mama and Agnes have not returned. Because at least if they have returned, they will clear the ground. Or praps they are staying in another part of Dukana. Awright, if it is so then I must go and look for them or anybody who can tell me something about what is happening. So I begin to walk everywhere in Dukana. All the doors of the houses were closed. Any many houses that have fallen down nobody was cleaning or removing the mud and the thatch or clearing the grass. As I am walking I will be shouting my name. Still nobody opens the door of their house. Ah-ah. What is happening?

In one house, I saw smoke coming from the roof. So I said somebody must be in that house cooking otherwise there cannot be smoke in the house. So I went to the door of the house and began to knock and to shout my name. I was shouting my name very loud and knocking on the door very loud. But nobody answered my call. I even wanted to broke the door and go inside. But after some time I changed my mind and continued to walk inside the town.

One time I saw one man walking towards me. I think I know the man very well. It is Bom. So I started to run so that I can get near him quickly. I was very happy because at least I have seen one Dukana man that I know and porson who can tell me everything. But do you know what happened? As soon as this man saw me, he turned away and began to run from me. I pursued him. But he ran very fast and disappeared. Ah-ah? Is it not Bom that I have seen that time that I came to Dukana in Manmuswak land rover? Was he not hiding in the forest drinking palmy and roasting yam? He did not run away from me that time. Why is he running away from me now? Look, I don't like what is happening at all.

So now I said that I will not walk in Dukana again. I must go back to the church and then I will think what I will do because I cannot stay in the church all the time and praps I cannot stay in Dukana again. To talk true I was not happy at all. And not just that I was not happy. I was very very sad at all. Because this is not what I was thinking all this time that I was looking for my mama in refugee camp or after the war have ended before I started to return. So I begin to walk small small, small small, with my eye on the ground to return to the church.

When I reached the church, I just lay on the ground and then sleep come catch me. I slept well well whether because I did not sleep in the night or because I am very tired I don't know. But anyway I sleep well well because by the time I open my eye, it was very very dark. And then I begin to see those people with lantern again walking with small bundle on their head going to the bad forest. This time I did not follow them because already I know where they are going. So plenty people are dying in Dukana. But what is killing them? Is it hunger or kwashiokor? No, it cannot be. Because if all these people did not die in compost pit refugee camp why should they die in Dukana after they have returned and there is plenty food because nobody have harvested the food during the war and now people do not have money to buy the food and anybody can eat anything that he likes many times in one day. So it must be juju. But who is using juju to kill everybody in Dukana? And why are they running from me?

I was still thinking this thing in my mind when I heard something like snake or cockroach or cat or tiger moving in the door of the church. I did not move or say anything. I just stayed where I was lying down quietly like tortoise because I do not want any bad thing to know that I am in that church and praps come to worry me. But I was only wasting my time because no sooner than a voice that I know very well shouted: "Whoever you are, whether ghost or spirit or man or juju, hiding in this church come out now and let me see you."

Ah-ah? Is this not the voice of Duzia the cripple man? I am sure that it is his voice. So I was very happy.

So I said "Duzia, voice of Dukana, I am your son, Sozaboy. I have returned from the war."

"Are you alive or dead?" is what Duzia asked next.

Wonderful. How can I be dead and I am sleeping in the church in Dukana?

"I am alive, my brother," is what I replied.

"If true true you are alive come here and let me see you with my own eyes," is what Duzia said next.

So I got up and began to walk towards the door. By this time day have begin to break small small so it was not very dark in the church. I can see Duzia sitting near the church door. I walked to him.

"Give me your hand let me hold you," is what Duzia said.

I gave him my hand.

"Now bend down and touch your toes."

I bend down and touch my toes.

"Call me by my name again."

So I said "Duzia what is this thing you are doing to me? Don't you know me again? Can't you hear my voice? I am Sozaboy, your own Sozaboy."

"It is so. True true you are not ghost or anything like that." This is what Duzia said.

"Did anybody say that I am ghost?" I asked him.

"Well, Sozaboy, juju smallpox, that is what I used to call you, and that is what you are, the things that are happening in Dukana these days, everybody must to be careful because things are not as they used to be. Sit down, Sozaboy, let me tell you."

"Is it so?" is what I asked. Then I sat near Duzia.

"Yes, Sozaboy, juju smallpox. Everything have changed," is what Duzia replied.

"I beg tell me."

"You see, since everybody returned from the war and the refugee camp, Dukana is different place. And I am telling you, because I like you very much as fine picken and fine young man concern, you must go away from Dukana one time."

"Is that so?" is all I was able to say.

I think you know what I was thinking by the time I heard this. How can I go away from Dukana just like that? Is it not my town again? And is it not my mama and my wife town? And if I go away where can I go that they will take somebody who have been driven away from his own town where they born him? But why are they driving me away?

I think Duzia know what I was thinking because he said to me: "Since the war ended and everybody came back, they are saying that you have already dead since the war started."

"But that is not true,' I replied.

"I am telling you what they said. They are saying that though you have dead, you turn to ghost and begin to worry everybody."

"Why?"

"Because you love your mother and your wife Agnes who were killed by bomb and since they have dead, you said that everybody in Dukana must die too."

"So my mama and my young wife Agnes were killed by bomb, is it?"

"Yes."

"When?"

"That time that bomb fell on Dukana the third time. They are the only people who were killed by bomb."

"But you did not tell me the other time when I came to see you in Dukana. And in fact, nobody have told me. Zaza did not tell me. Terr Kole did not tell me. Chief Birabee and Pastor Barika did not tell me."

"Sozaboy, you are not small boy again. You know that in this town, nobody can tell you about dead people first. Nobody likes to carry bad news. That is why they did not tell you."

"So my mama and my Agnes have dead?"

"Yes."

I just bend my head down and begin to cry. The water was falling plenty plenty from my eye. And the pain inside my heart was very very bad. I cry for my young wife with J.J.C. and for my mama who born me. Oh God, why have you punished me like this?

"Sozaboy, don't cry again. Man cannot cry like picken, you know."

"Duzia, I beg you, leave me alone. I beg you," I said crying.

"I cannot leave you alone," Duzia said. "Because I am your friend. You see, Dukana people are saying that although you have already dead, you have become ghost and sometime you can appear as proper porson and go to where Dukana people are staying and begin to ask for your mama and your wife Agnes."

"Is it so?"

"Yes. And if you do not see your wife and your mama, then you will begin to kill the people. That is why when you were in refugee camp where Dukana people were staying, plenty of Dukana people begin to die like ant."

"Is it so?" I asked.

"Yes. And even when Chief Birabee and Pastor Barika wanted to take soza to arrest you, you disappeared one time and since that time nobody have seen you again."

"Is that so?"

"Yes. And now that the war have ended, you have returned again as ghost to Dukana to worry those who have not yet dead."

"True?"

"Yes. And now you have put very bad disease in the town to kill everybody. Sozaboy, this disease that you have put, we cannot understand it. It is not like smallpox which used to make small small pit in man face. This new juju disease will just make porson go latrine plenty times and then the porson will die. Plenty people are just dying like that, like fly."

"True?"

"Yes. And every time, whether morning, afternoon or night, your ghost will just be walking inside the town shouting your name, Sozaboy, Sozaboy. And calling other people name. And asking them for your mama and your wife. And anybody that you ask or call their name in the evening, he or she must die by night time after going plenty latrine."

"Is it so?" I said.

"Yes. So we have gone to see juju about this thing. And the juju have told us that unless we kill your ghost, everybody in Dukana must die. So, we looked for money and seven white goats and seven white monkey *blokkus* and seven alligator pepper and seven bundles of plantain and seven young young girls that we will give to the juju to make sacrifice."

"Is it so?" I asked.

"Yes. And the juju have told us that seven days after he have made the sacrifice, you will return from the place where you have been staying, and then they will bury you proper so that your ghost cannot return to Dukana."

"True?"

"Yes. The juju said that your ghost is moving round killing everybody because when you were killed in the war, they did not bury you proper. And anybody that they do not bury proper in the ground with drink and dance after he have already dead, surely his ghost must move round like porson wey no get house until they bury him like proper man."

As Duzia was saying this thing, I am telling you I was shaking with fear. Because he have told me true true that one, my mama and my Agnes have already dead; and two, if Dukana people see me they will kill me and bury me. Because if porson who does not know Dukana people hear this tory, they will just laugh and say that it is nonsense tory. But Dukana is not like that. The people are wicked more than. Anything can happen in that town. And anything which concern death, they will believe it if juju tell them something. Because porson does not just die in Dukana. Somebody must kill any porson who have dead before he can die. And now as many people are dying from this disease that they do not understand and no medicine to treat them, they must look for a native way to stop people from dying whether it will work oh or it will not work. And after they have all make plan to kill anybody, they will just kill that porson and nobody in this world will know. Because nobody in that town will talk or tell police or anybody.

So I said to myself that if I did not die for Iwoama and I did not die in refugee camp and I did not die that time that Manmuswak took me from prison to shoot me and the other prisoners, God forbid that I will die when the war have already finish. And even if I will die sef, I cannot just stay in that Dukana and allow people to come and kill me like goat or rat or ant when I am Sozaboy. So now I just think to myself that as Duzia is cripple man, he cannot follow me and if I run away the only thing he can do is to hala and call people and since they are all fearing and sitting in their rotten house with every door closed, they will not hear him. And even sef, I do not think that Duzia will shout because if he shout and the people come out and they do not see me, they will say that Duzia is talking with ghost therefore he is very bad man and they can even kill him one time.

So now I just get up from where I was sitting. I did not say one word to Duzia again. I just get up and begin to go. As I was going, I looked at the place where my mama house used to stand. And tears began to drop like rain from my eyes. I walked quickly from my own town Dukana and in fact I did not know where I was going.

And as I was going, I was just thinking how the war have spoiled my town Dukana, uselessed many people, killed many others, killed my mama and my wife, Agnes, my beautiful young wife with J.J.C. and now it have made me like porson wey get leprosy because I have no town again.

And I was thinking how I was prouding before to go to soza and call myself Sozaboy. But now if anybody say anything about war or even fight, I will just run and run and run and run and run. Believe me yours sincerely.

GLOSSARY

abi	or; is it?
abi the girl no dey shame?	or is the girl not shy?
Ajuwaya	As you were
all two and two pence	all the same; alike
anmal	animal
ashbottom	see *kotuma ashbottom*
ashewo	prostitute
as him hand reach	according to his ability
assault	offence. See also *giving me assault*
as some thing used to be	maybe (literally, *as matters could turn out*)
babar me	cut my hair; shave my head
before before	prior to this; previously
big big English/big big grammar	tedious, erudite arguments or statements in standard English
big eye	see *get big eye*
blokkus	testicles
bobby	breasts
bogey	see *short man bogey*
borku	plentiful
born	to give birth to
'bottom belly'	title of a popular record
byforce	rape
called another man's wife	committed adultery
chooking	piercing, injecting
chooking needle	syringe
chop	to eat; food
chop big big bribe	accept huge bribes
chop money	food allowance
commot	come out; go out
commot for garage	leave the garage
cooleh	see *take make small cooleh*
corple	corporal
country	ethnic group
cunny	trick; cunning

cut	beat
cut our heart	frighten us
dabara	let go
death for your doormouth	death on your doorstep
dey for house	stay at home
D.O.	District Officer
does not get mouth	has no rights (especially of speech)
drink don begin turn-turn for my eye	I was getting tipsy
drink hot	take alcoholic drink
eba	a food made by mixing *gari* with water
enter inside pepper soup	get into trouble
face tight	frowning
fine baby	pretty girl
fit	can; to be able
form fool	make a silly mistake; fool around
free-born	citizen
gari	a local food, powdery like rice. See also *water don pass gari*.
get belly	become pregnant
get big eye	be ambitious; greedy
ginkana	locally brewed gin
give you moless	molest you
giving me assault	insulting me
God no gree bad thing	God forbid!
gra gra	see *make gra-gra*
gratulate	congratulate
gree	allow, agree
hala	holler, shout
heavy	Untranslatable as used here. Denotes pride of the speaker in foregoing event
helele	thoroughly; properly
hibatension	hypertension
him hand reach	see under *as him hand reach*
his face tight	he was frowning
his trouble was more than	his problems trebled

hold joke	pretend
Hopen udad mas/Hoping udad mas!	Open order march
hot drink	alcoholic drink
incharger	supervisor; commander
J.J.C.	Johnny Just Come (denotes a girl with lovely pointed breasts)
juju	medicine man, shaman, magician; magical
kain	kind
Kampala	a guardroom (nickname)
Kana	a language of the Ogoni people of Nigeria
khaki	pair of shorts
knack	talk; throw
knack tory	to gossip; chat
koboko	horsewhip
kotuma ashbottom	customary court bailiff
kpongoss	ancient; aged
lai lai	at all
lomber	number
long throat	greed
make gra–gra	be unduly quarrelsome
make stronghead	be obstinate
making yanga	being unduly proud
mala	bald; see *shave my head mala*
mambo–jambo	nonsense
man	penis
man must wak	a man must live (eat) by whatever means
massa	master; boss
Mene them	Mene and others
mess up their senior commando	disgrace themselves
moless	see *give you moless*
more than	worse
mouth	see *does not get mouth*
mumu	idiot
na je-je	it's stylish
na waya oh	see *this girl na waya-oh*

ngwo ngwo	mutton in pepper soup (a specially prepared delicacy)
no gree am	see *she no gree am*
no gree me go	did not agree to let me go
oga	boss (from 'ogre')
okporoko	stockfish
okro	okra
old pass myself plenty	much older than me
oyibo	white man
palaver	trouble
palmy	palm wine
particulars	bits and pieces of mutton
people are wicked more than	the people are most wicked
people plenty for am	there are many people there
pepper	See *enter inside pepper soup* and *see pepper*
persy	dignity, composure. See also *preserve their persy*
picken	child
picture on the hand	see under *with picture*
pit	trench
preserve their persy	maintain their equanimity
prison	imprison
prouding	boasting; vaunting
P.T.	physical training shorts
Qua shun!	Squad shun (Attention!)
rapa	loincloth. See *woman rapa*
rope	insignia of office (lance corporal, one rope; corporal, two ropes; sergeant, three ropes)
sabi	to know
sand-sand	sand; dust
San Mazor	Sergeant Major
Sarogua	ancestral spirit, guardian of Dukana sergeant
sarzent	sergeant
see pepper	see red
sef	even
senior commando	see *mess up their senior commando*
service	sales person; steward/stewardess

sha	truly
shame	blush
shave my head mala	clean-shave me
she no gree am	she did not allow him to make love to her
short man bogey	an exclamation denoting admiration for a powerful short man (in this case, a gun)
show me pepper	give me trouble; cause me grief
Simple Defence	Civil Defence
small	a little
SMOG	save me o God
solope arms	slope arms
some thing used to be	see *as some thing used to be*
some time	perhaps
soso	mostly; entirely
sotey	until
soza/sozaman	soldier
staat eese/stand at hais	stand at ease
stiff him hand by himself	stood to attention
stronghead	obstinacy
take make small cooleh	enjoy oneself with
take me make ye-ye	make fun of me
Tan Papa dere	Stand properly there
terprita	interpreter
thick man	tough cookie
this girl na waya-oh	this girl is something else
throway	throw away
tief	steal
titis	pretty girls
tombo	palm wine
tory	see *knack tory*
tory don worwor	the worst has happened (literally, *the story has worsened*)
toto	vagina
traffic	traffic policeman
trouble	see *his trouble was more than*
Tufia	spitting action (onomatopoeia)

turn-turn for my eye	see *drink don turn-turn for my eye*
two and two pence	see *all two and two pence*
Udad arms	Order arms
ugbalugba	problem
very before	right before me
VIO	Vehicle Inspection Officer
wahala	trouble, hullabaloo
water don pass gari	matters have come to a head (Where there's more water than gari, the resulting paste is virtually inedible.)
waya	tough (literally, wire; so as tough as wire); something else
waya-oh	see *this girl na waya-oh*
wetin	what (literally, *what thing*)
wetin call	you name it
wey	who
whackies	food
whether whether	no matter what
which one I dey	Untranslatable; roughly: *What's my role?*
whosai	where (literally, *what side*)
wicked more than	see *people are wicked more than*
with picture on the hand	with an emblem on the sleeve
woman rapa	a womaniser; one who dotes on women
wor-wor pass	worse than
wuruwuru	chicanery; cheating
yafu-yafu	hopeless
yanga	pride. See also *making yanga*
yarse	arse
yekpe	useless
yeye	doomed. See also *take me make yeye*
yeye man	n'er-do-well

Other Titles Available

Longman African Writers

Tides	I Okpewho	0 582 10276 6
Of Men and Ghosts	K Aidoo	0 582 22871 9
Flowers and Shadows	B Okri	0 582 03536 8
Violence	F Iyayi	0 582 00240 0
The Victims	I Okpewho	0 582 00241 9
Call Me Not a Man	M Matshoba	0 582 00242 7
The Beggar's Strike	A Sowfall	0 582 00243 5
Dilemma Of a Ghost/Anowa	A A Aidoo	0 582 00244 3
Our Sister Killjoy	A A Aidoo	0 582 00391 1
No Sweetness Here	A A Aidoo	0 582 00393 8
The Marriage of Anansewa/Edufa	E Sutherland	0 582 00245 1
The Cockroach Dance	M Mwangi	0 582 00392 X
Muriel At Metropolitan	M Tlali	0 582 01657 6
The Children of Soweto	M Mzamane	0 582 01680 0
A Son Of The Soil	W Katiyo	0 582 02656 3
The Stillborn	Z Alkali	0 582 02657 1
The Life of Olaudah Equiano	P Edwards	0 582 03070 6
Sundiata	D T Niane	0 582 64259 0
The Last Duty	I Okpewho	0 582 78535 9
Tales of Amadou Koumba	B Diop	0 582 78587 1
Native Life South Africa	S Plaatje	0 582 78589 8
Hungry Flames	M Mzamane	0 582 78590 1
Scarlet Song	M Ba	0 582 78595 2
Fools	N Ndebele	0 582 78621 5
Master and Servant	D Mulwa	0 582 78632 0
The Park	J Matthews	0 582 04080 9
Man Pass Man	N Mokoso	0 582 01681 9
Hurricane of Dust	A Djoleto	0 582 01682 7
Heroes	F Iyayi	0 582 78603 7
Loyalties	A Maja-Pearce	0 582 78628 2
Sugarcane With Salt	J Ng'ombe	0 582 05205 1
Study Guide to 'Scarlet Song'	M Ba	0 582 21979 5

All these titles are available from your local bookseller, or he can order them for you. For further information on these titles, and on study guides available, contact your local Longman agent or Longman International Education, Longman Group Limited, Longman House, Burnt Mill, Harlow, Essex, CM20 2JE, England.